TOURING ATLAS
South Afri

AND BOTSWANA | MOZAMBIQUE | NAMIBIA | ZIMBABWE

CONTENTS

South Africa : Main Map pages and Key 2-3

Cape Town, Clanwilliam and Swellendam	4
Knysna, Oudtshoorn and Beaufort West	5
Port Elizabeth, Graaff-Reinet and Grahamstown	6
East London, King William's Town and Mthatha (Umtata)	7
Namaqualand and Alexander Bay	8
Upington, Kenhardt and Calvinia	9
Prieska, Griquatown and Carnarvon	10
Bloemfontein, Kimberley and Middelburg	11
Lesotho, Harrismith and Mthatha (Umtata)	12
Durban, Ulundi and Port Edward	13
Namib Desert, Ai-Ais Richtersveld Transfrontier Park	14
Kgalagadi Transfrontier Park and Karasburg	15
Kalahari Desert and Kuruman	16
Mafikeng, Vryburg and Welkom	17
Gauteng, Ermelo and Harrismith	18
Swaziland, Nelspruit and Ulundi	19
Gaborone, Palapye and Mokopane (Potgietersrus)	20
Polokwane (Pietersburg) and Kruger National Park	21

South Africa : Areas of Interest in detail and Key 22-23

The Cape Peninsula	24-25
Stellenbosch, Paarl and Franschhoek Vineyards	26-27
Wine Region of the Western Cape	28-29
Western Cape	30-31
The Wilderness	32-33
Tsitsikamma National Park	34-35
Port Elizabeth and East London	36-37
KwaZulu-Natal's South Coast	38-39
KwaZulu-Natal's North Coast	40-41
uKhahlamba-Drakensberg Park	42-43
Kruger National Park	44-45
Pilanesberg and Magaliesberg Region	46-47
The Witwatersrand	48-49

City and Administrative Centres and Key 50

Cape Town and The Waterfront	51
Pretoria	52
Johannesburg	53
Bloemfontein and Environs	54
Durban and Environs	55
Pietermaritzburg and Ulundi	56
East London, King William's Town and Bhisho	57
Port Elizabeth and Environs	58
Kimberley and Environs	59
Mafikeng and Environs	60
Nelspruit and Environs	61
Polokwane (Pietersburg) and Environs	62

Neighbouring Countries and Key 63

Namibia	64-65
Windhoek – Namibia	66
Etosha National Park – Namibia	67
Botswana	68
Gaborone and Okavango Delta – Botswana	69
Zimbabwe – Victoria Falls and Hwange National Park	70-71
Harare and Bulawayo – Zimbabwe	72
Nyanga National Park and Great Zimbabwe	73
Mozambique	74
Maputo and Beira – Mozambique	75

SUNBIRD PUBLISHERS

First edition 2000
Reprinted in 2002, 2003, 2004, 2005, 2006
Second edition 2008
Sunbird Publishers (Pty) Ltd
P O Box 6836, Roggebaai, 8012
Cape Town, South Africa
e-mail: Sunbird@media24.co.za

www.sunbirdpublishers.co.za

Registration number: 1984/003543/07

Copyright © published edition Sunbird Publishers
Cartographer & Designer John Hall
Cover design by Peter Bosman
Reproduced by Resolution, Cape Town
Printed and bound by Tien Wah Press (Pte) Ltd, Singapore

ISBN 978-1-919938-83-7

Please note that where major town names have changed we have included the previous name in brackets as road signs may still show old name.

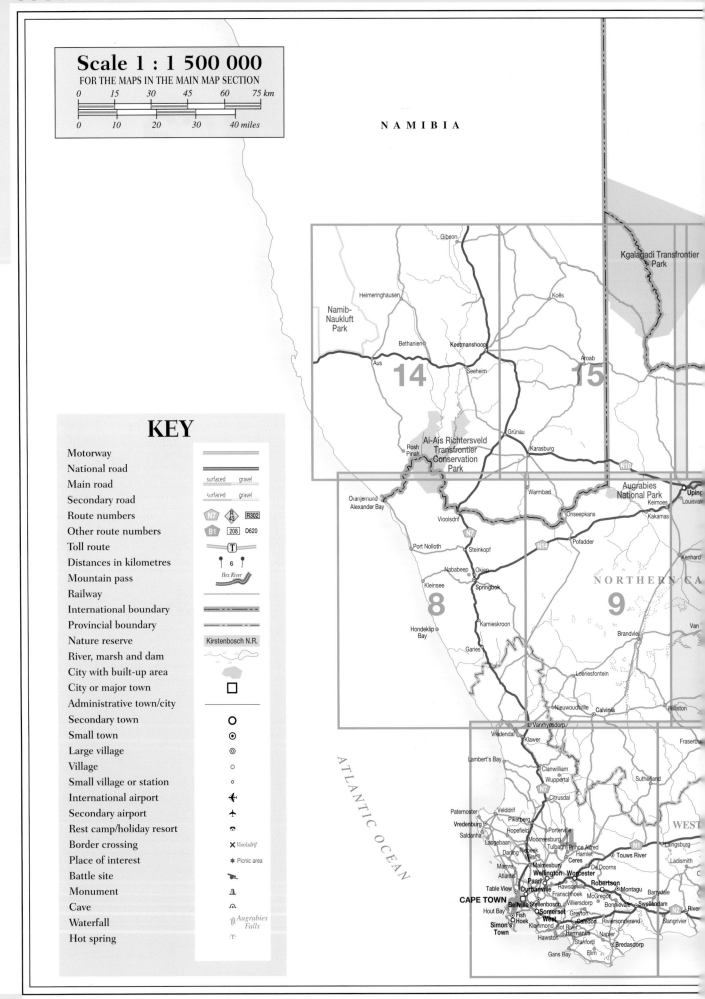

Scale 1 : 1 500 000
FOR THE MAPS IN THE MAIN MAP SECTION

0	15	30	45	60	75 km

0	10	20	30	40 miles

KEY

Motorway	
National road	surfaced gravel
Main road	surfaced gravel
Secondary road	
Route numbers	N7 R43 R302
Other route numbers	B1 208 D620
Toll route	T
Distances in kilometres	6
Mountain pass	Hex River
Railway	
International boundary	
Provincial boundary	
Nature reserve	Kirstenbosch N.R.
River, marsh and dam	
City with built-up area	
City or major town	▢
Administrative town/city	
Secondary town	○
Small town	◉
Large village	◎
Village	○
Small village or station	○
International airport	✈
Secondary airport	✈
Rest camp/holiday resort	
Border crossing	✕ Vioolsdrif
Place of interest	✳ Picnic area
Battle site	
Monument	⚱
Cave	⌓
Waterfall	Augrabies Falls
Hot spring	⋎

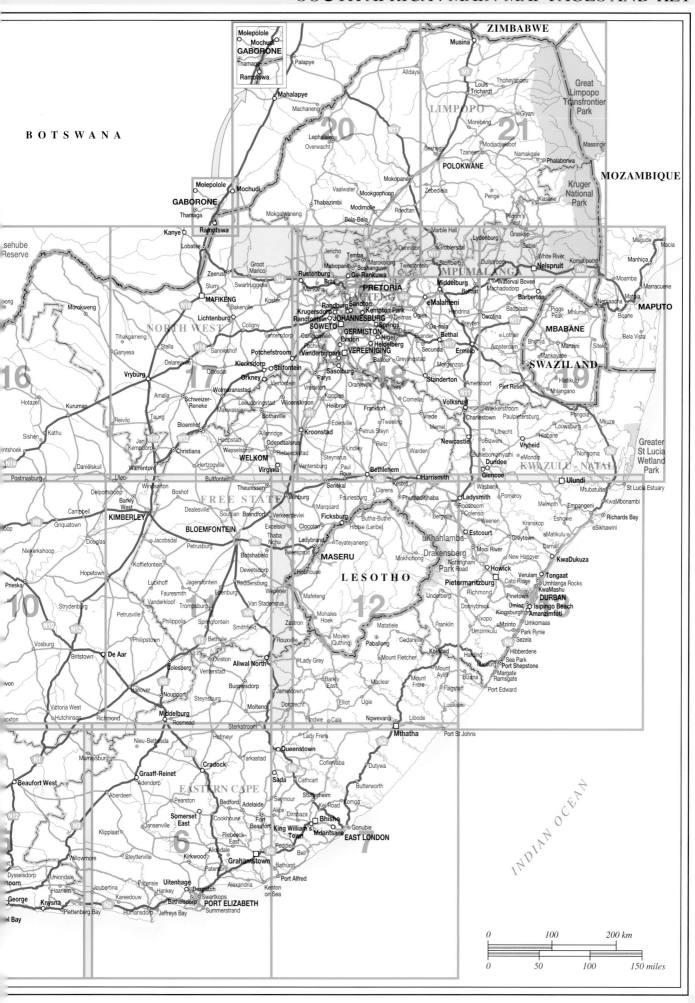

continued on page 9

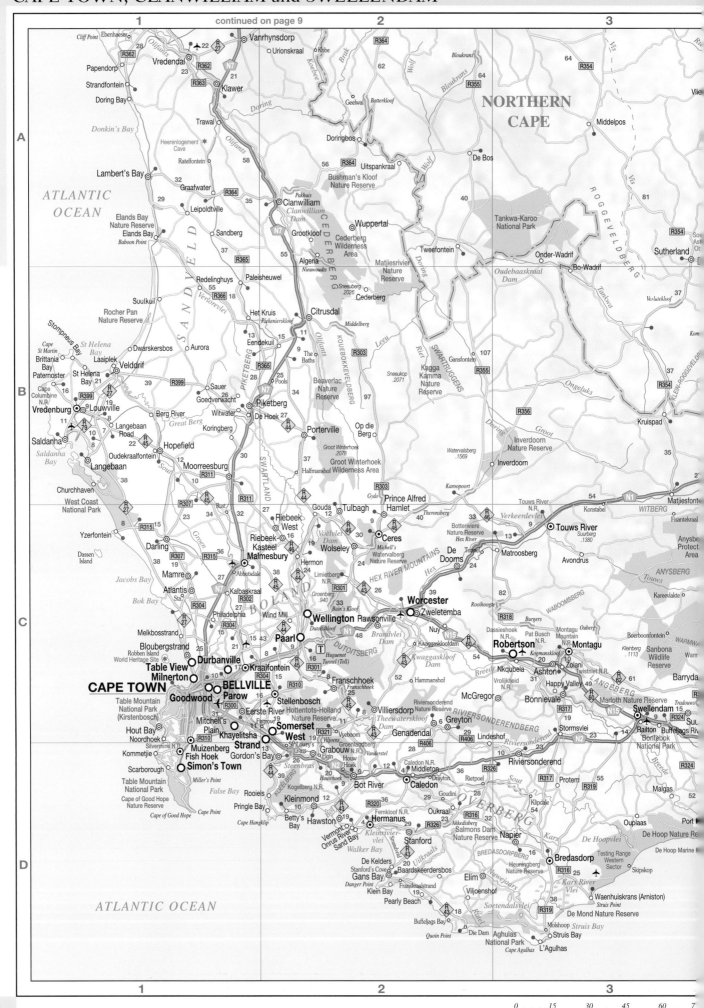

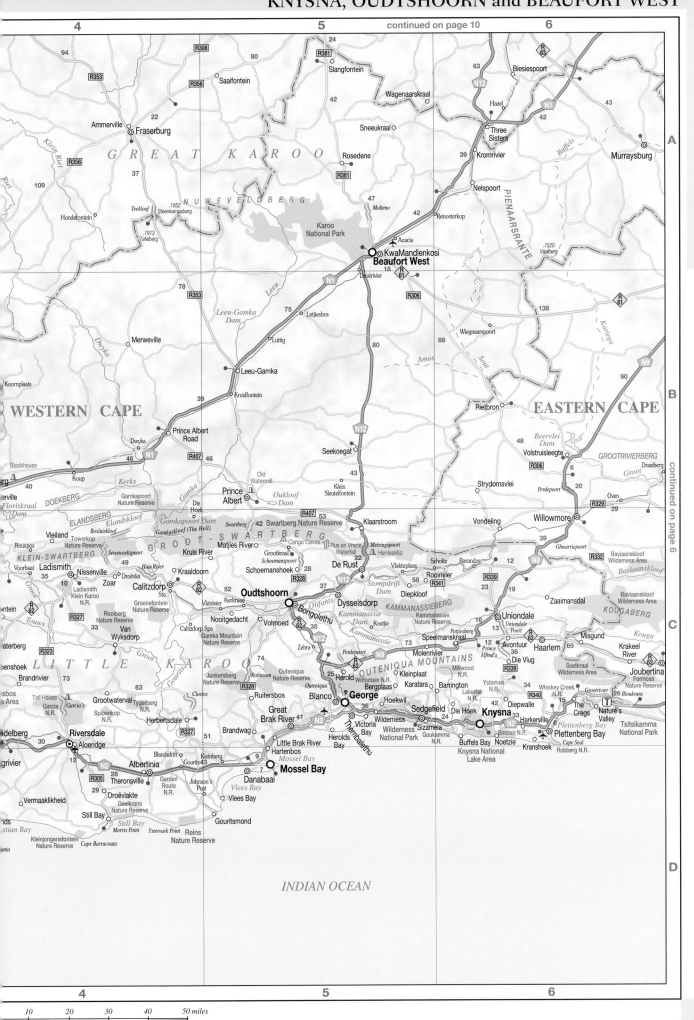

continued on page 10

continued on page 6

INDIAN OCEAN

WESTERN CAPE

EASTERN CAPE

10   20   30   40   50 miles

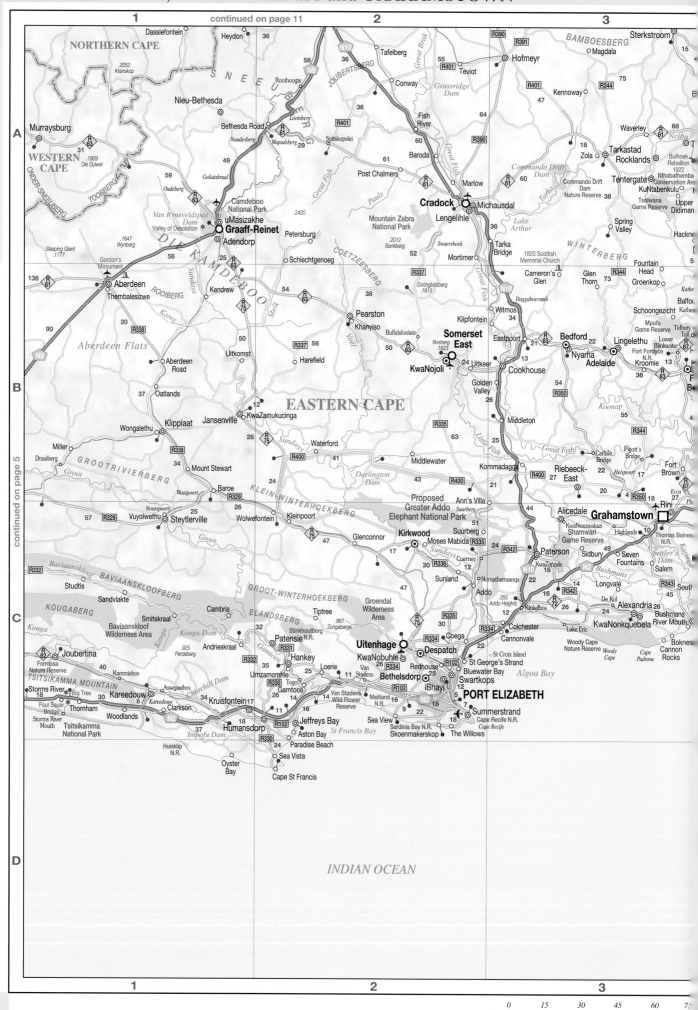

continued on page 11

continued on page 5

INDIAN OCEAN

0   15   30   45   60   75

4 5 continued on page 12 6

Zitapaleni Hali Askeaton Zadungweni Bhaziya R61 53 **Mthatha** Ngxanga Lokweni R61 Port St Johns
oring Lady Nyalasa Ngcobo Coghlan Komkhulu Bidiza Lutsheko Silaka Dick King
R392 Frere Bukwana Gcina Sikobeni 32 eXwili Ngangelizwe Nzwakazi Ngqeleni Old Thombo Silaka Nature
R359 Cacadu KuMbaxa 51 KwaBityi 54 Qota Jojweni Sijungqwini Bunting Notintsila Umgazi Reserve
Xonxa Nyongwana KwaMzola Mjanyana Clarkebury Jojweni Nkumandeni Mouth Hluleka Nature
Dam Lubisi KwaMadikana Seru Halane Qunu KwaZulu Ntsundwane Reserve
Driver's Dam Luxeni Mayireni 20 Hange 5 Ndlunkulu Qokama Bityi Mqanduli Ntibane Hluleka
Drift Tsojana Hange Tsomo N2 Mbashe Itayi 32 Gengqe Old Morley
Queenstown Qamata 42 Cofimvaba Hlobo Dutywa Mvezo KwaNdelane Elliotdale Manzi Mthatha Mouth
eZibeleni 18 Rwantsana St Mark's R61 Xolobe Tsomo Mjula eSihlabeni Tyelekebende KwaNokatana Coffee Bay
Ilinge Bholothwa 24 KwaFanti 53 Xilinxa Mangwane 36 eNtshatshongo Khamisa Hole in the Wall
Tylden Mangobomvu Dam KwaJama Hobeni
hittlesea 41 Waqu 48 Mbalakweza Esigadini KuMaya Nocwane
humleni R351 Nciba Mangondini Ibeka Willowvale Dwesa The Haven
44 Catholic Toleni Head Ndabakazi Mandluntsha Dwesa-Cwebe Marine Reserve
Upper Cathcart Cross 46 Butterworth Jujura
Chilton Katikati Bholo Centuli Kabakazi Qora Mouth
R345 1820 Manubi Mazeppa Bay
Settler's N6 48 Toyise 34 Mgwali Centane Takazi Cebe
48 Milestone Thomas Wriggleswade Kubusi Qumra Mpethu Nxaxo Mouth
Hogsback River Gubu Dam Bleakmoor R63 Qolora Mouth
AMATHOLE Stutterheim R352 Draaibosch 20 Kei Mouth
Keiskammahoek Gwiligwili Dontsa Cumakala 1877 48 Morgan's Bay
Tyume River 37 Kubusi 17 40 KwaMahomba R349 Haga-Haga
R345 Red Hill Woodlands 26 Mooiplaas Chintsa Mouth
Dam Sandile Dam Frankfort Kei Macleantown Chintsa West
Ntselamanzi 21 22 Road Kwetyana 23 Glen Muir
Fort Hare R352 KwaMangati 28 Macleantown 31 Queensberry Bay
ledrift 63 R63 22 **Bhisho** Berlin 24 Fort 12 Gonubie Kwelera Nature Reserve
40 Dimbaza 17 Jackson 17 **Beacon Bay**
Drift Ngcabasa **King William's** Ndevana N6 **EAST LONDON** INDIAN OCEAN
reserve 1835 **Town** Zwelitsha Mdantsane N2 Gompo Town
ast R345 Milkwood Qawukeni 53 R346 Fort Pato 12 Cove Rock
Tree 29 Sittingbourne N.R. Bridle Winterstrand
26 1841 Chalumna 18 Drift Gulu N.R.
mmittees Watch Tower R72 19 Dam Kidd's Beach
R345 17 Cross R347 Christmas Rock
Peddie Roads 43 Kayser's Beach
N2 Magqazeni Bodiam
Nobumba eMahlubini Bell 5 Bodium
Fraser's KwaMpeko Gcinisa Hamburg
Camp 38 Fallodon Wesley
Mtati Shaw R72 Mpekweni
Park Great Fish Point
lukhanyo 27
kwenkwezi Kleinemonde
Port
Alfred

Mountain Zebra National Park near Cradock

NAMAQUALAND and ALEXANDER BAY

continued on page 14

1

Namib

DIAMOND AREA
(RESTRICTED ENTRANCE)

Orange

2

Ai-Ais Richtersveld
Transfrontier Conservation
Park

Vineyard
✦ Aussenkehr

Kuboes

C13

3

22

D316

13

D213

D208

D2

NAMIBIA

D208

B1

41

Oranjemund
× Beauvalion
Beesbank
Alexander Bay (permit only)
14
Alexander Bay

Alexander Bay

Noordoewer
Kotzeshoop
Vioolsdrif
Vioolsdrif

D208

Orange

D292

Eksteenfontein

Goodhouse

Wreck Point

84

70

Lekkersing

A

N7

B

North Point
Port Nolloth
South Point
McDougall's
Bay

Wedge Point

95   R382

Anenous
Steinkopf

Bulletrap

49

64

N14

*ATLANTIC
OCEAN*

38

Buffels

Lang Bay

Grootmis
Kleinsee

33
Buffelsbank
R355

Nigramoep

Nababeep
Bergsig
Springbok

Concordia

Okiep

Carolusberg
Goegap
Nature Reserve

47

69

Melkbos Point

Buffelsrivier
Spektakel

32

Komaggas

25

Messelpad

Burke's

Gamoep

N A M A Q U A L A N D

Namaqua
National Park

43

Kamassies

Rooifontein

51

Skulpfontein Point

Koingnaas

Soebatsfontein

N7

Bailey's

Kamieskroon

Leliefontein

Platbakkies

C

Doctor's Bay

Hondeklip
Bay

Spoegrivier

21

Kharkams

K A M I E S B E R G

Witwater

R35

Wallekraal

27   *Studer's*

Swart-Doring

Strandfontein Point   *Bitter*
Plat Bay

Soutfontein

Garies

Groen

Nariep

62

64

R358

Groenriviersmond

Island Point

Kotzesrus

Rietpoort

N7

Biesiesfontein

Bitterfontein

21

Blougat

WEST
CAP

Nuwerus

29

H A R D E V E L D

Komkans

Brand-se-Baai

Voëlklip

Landplaas

R363

28

Skaapvlei

Duiwegat

28

Koekenaap

Beeswater

Lutzville

R362

Cliff Point   Ebenhaeser

Olifants

28

D

Augrabies Falls National Park near Upington

continued on page 4

1   **2**   **3**

0   15   30   45   60   75

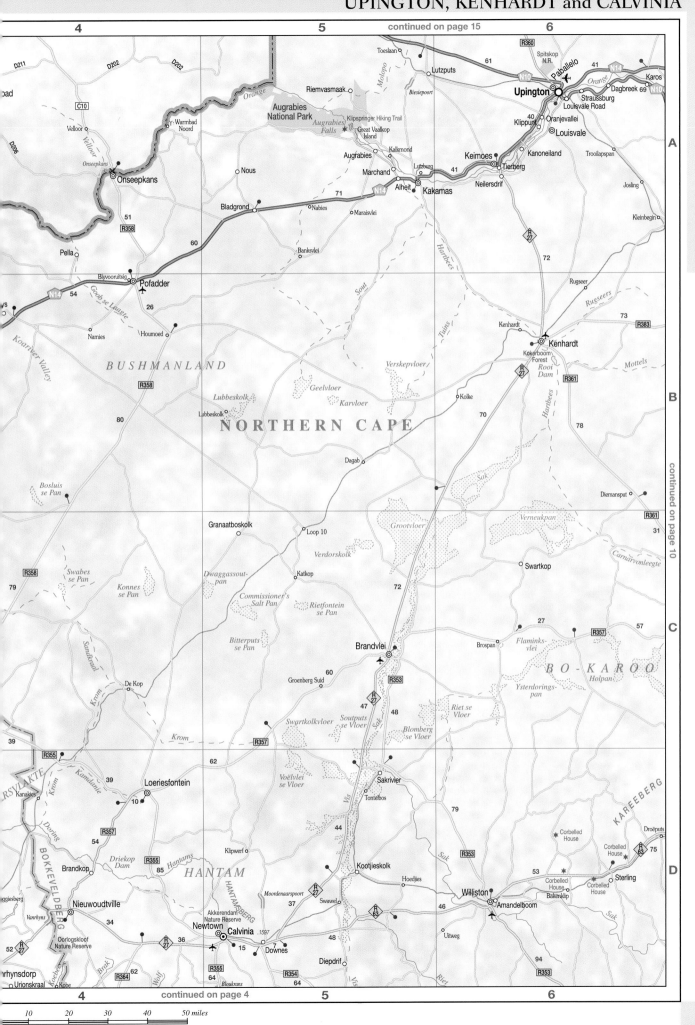

continued on page 15

continued on page 10

continued on page 4

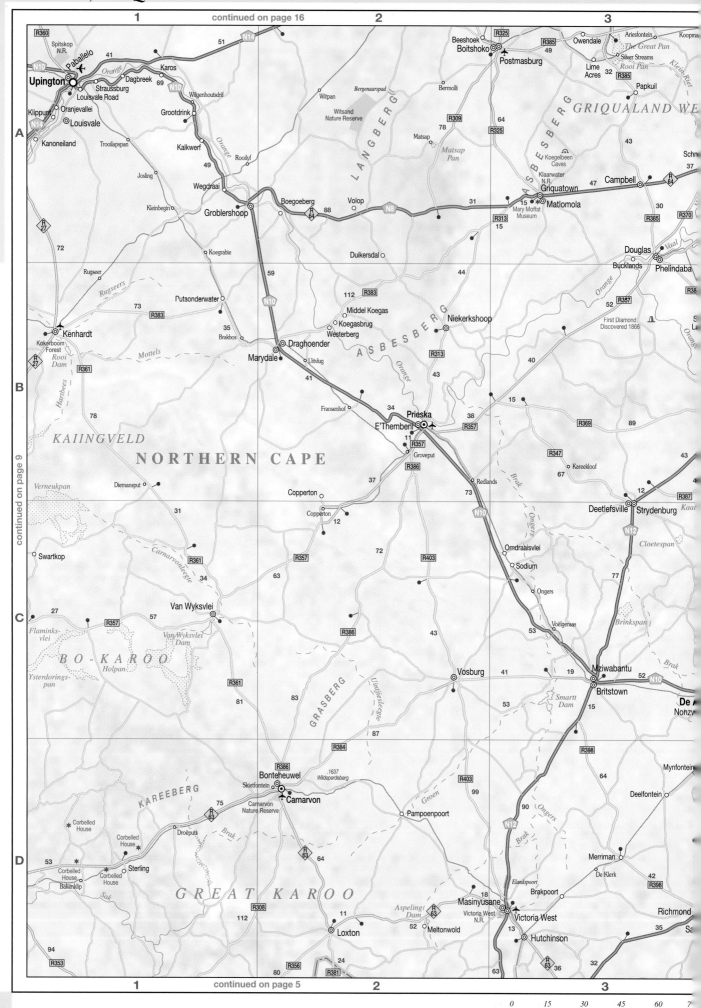

continued on page 16

continued on page 9

continued on page 5

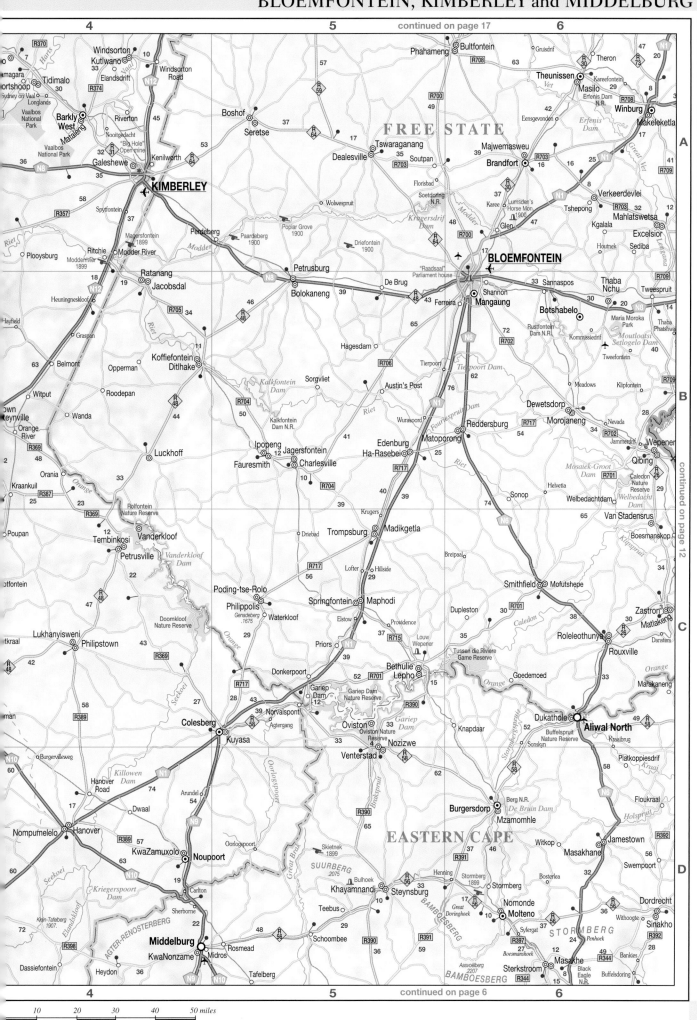

continued on page 17

continued on page 6

continued on page 12

LESOTHO, HARRISMITH and MTHATHA (UMTATA)

continued on page 18

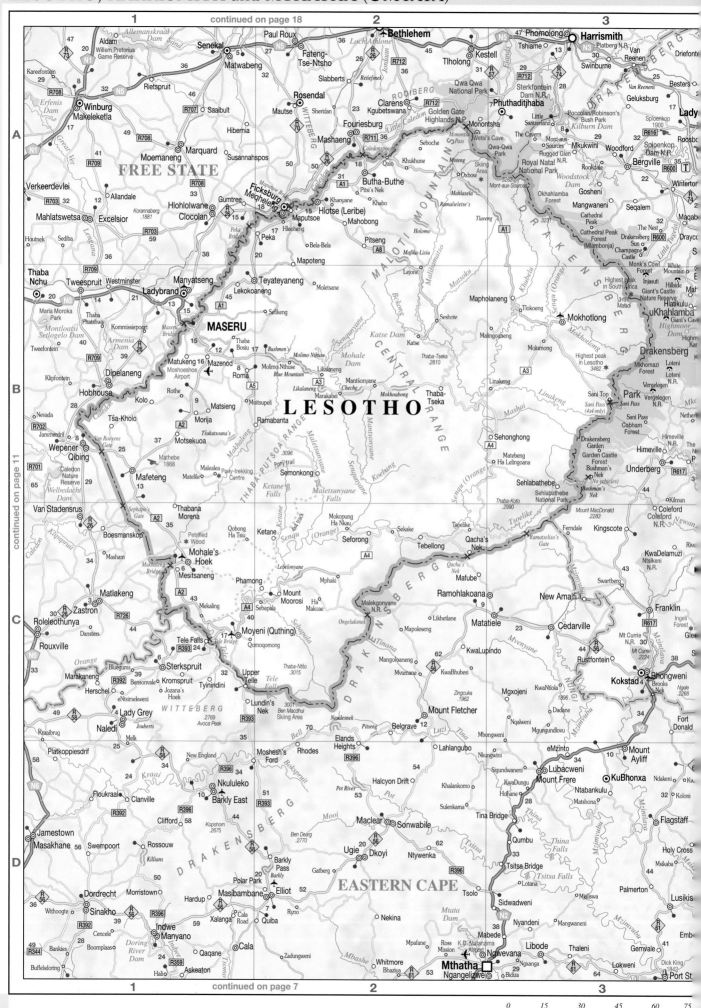

continued on page 11

continued on page 7

12

FREE STATE

LESOTHO

EASTERN CAPE

0 15 30 45 60 75

continued on page 19

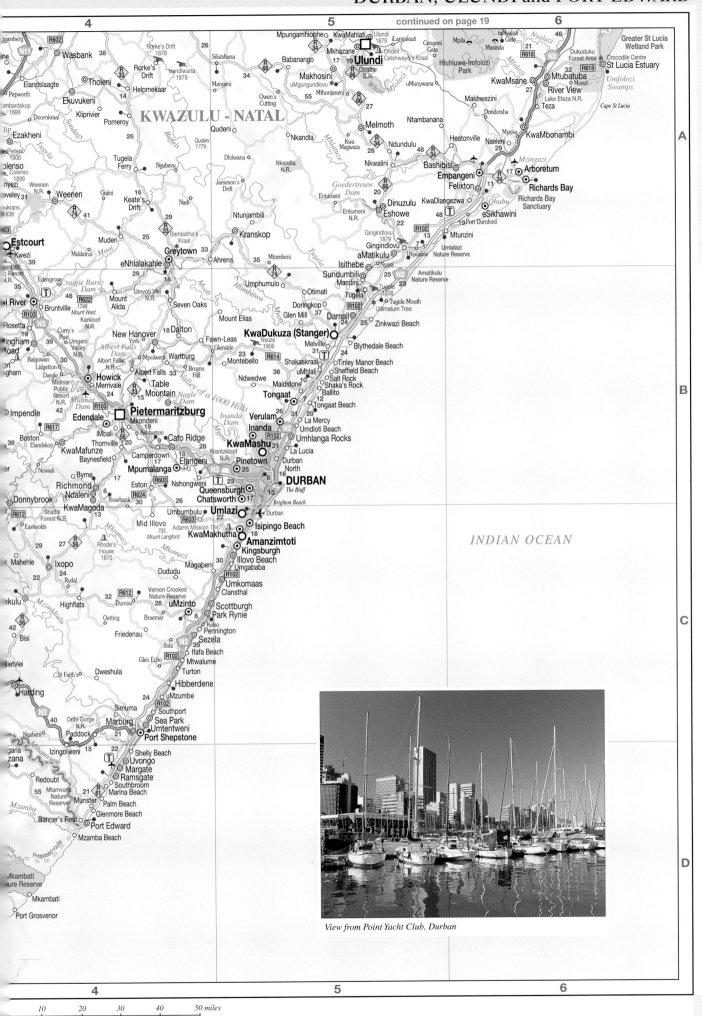

View from Point Yacht Club, Durban

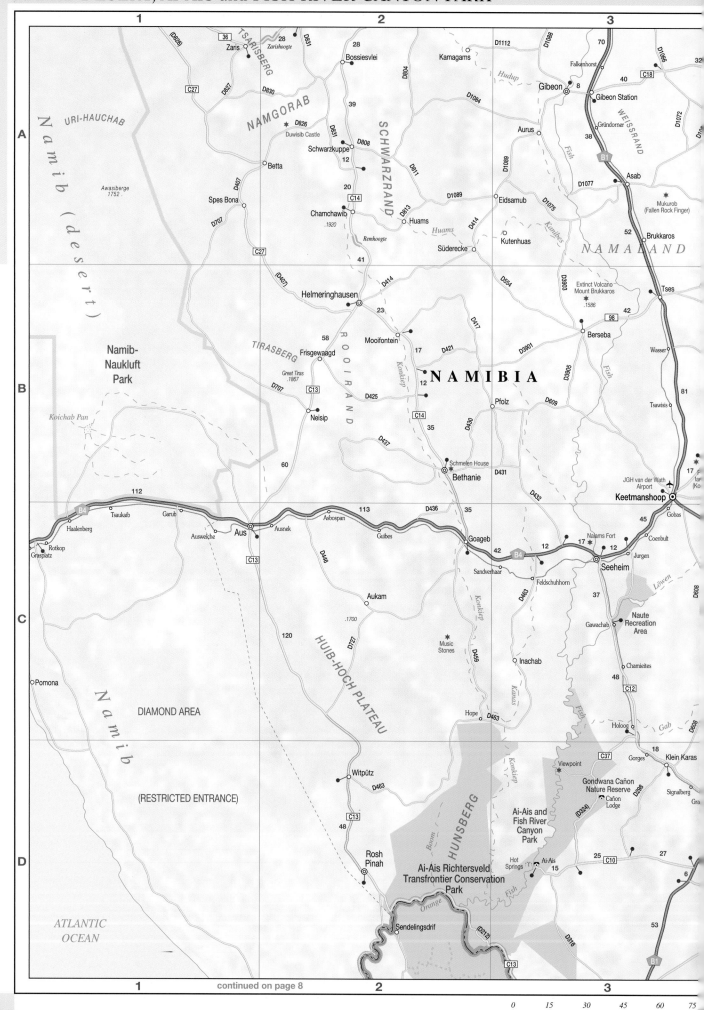

continued on page 8

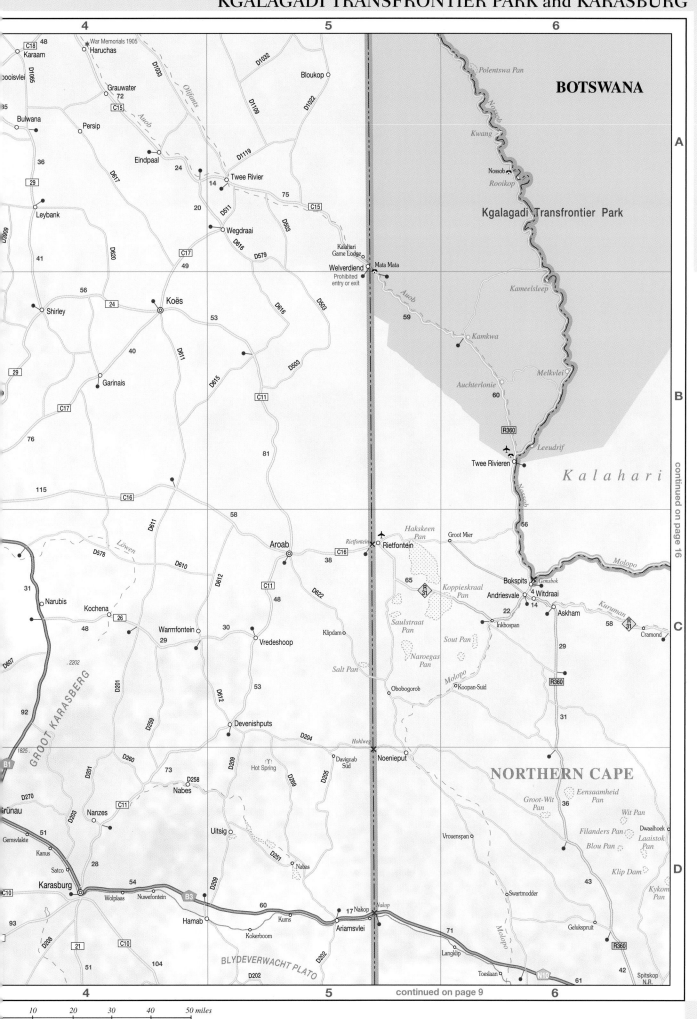

continued on page 16

continued on page 9

BOTSWANA

Polentswa Pan

Nossob

Kwang

Rooikop

Kgalagadi Transfrontier Park

Kameelsleep

Auob

59

Kamkwa

Melkvlei

Auchterlonie

60

R360

Leeudrif

Twee Rivieren

Kalahari

Nossob

56

Hakskeen Pan

Rietfontein Rietfontein

Groot Mier

38

C16

65

R31

Koppieskraal Pan

Bokspits *Gemsbok*

Andriesvale 4 Witdraai

22   14

Askham

Kuruman

58   R31

Cramond

Saulstraat Pan

Inkbospan

29

R360

31

Sout Pan

Naroegas Pan

Salt Pan

Molopo

Obobogorob

Koopan-Suid

Molopo

NORTHERN CAPE

Davignab Süd

Noenieput

Hot Spring

Hohlweg

Groot-Wit Pan   36

Eensaamheid Pan

Wit Pan

Filanders Pan

Dwaalhoek

Laaistok Pan

Blou Pan

Vrouenspan

Klip Dam

43

Kykom Pan

Swartmodder

Gelukspruit

R360

Nabes

Nanzes

Uitsig

Nabas

Hamab   Kums   Kokerboom

17 Nakop / Nakop

Ariamsvlei

71

Langklip

Molopo

N10

Toeslaan

61   42   Spitskop N.R.

Karasburg

Wolplaas   Nuwefontein

B3

60

BLYDEVERWACHT PLATO

D202

Kanus

Satco   28

51

Gemsvlakte

C10

93

D208   21   C10   51   104

Grünau

D270

D203

54

51

Groot Karasberg

B1   1825

92

D607

31

Narubis

Kochena   26

48

Warmfontein

29

Vredeshoop

30   Klipdam

48   D622   53

Devenishputs   D204

73   D258

D260   D201   D259   D612

D209   D269   D205   D251   D202

Aroab

C16

C11

D610   D612   D611   D578

2202

58

81

115

C16

76

C17

Koës

24

56

Shirley

Garinais

29

40

53

D611   D615   D616   D503

C11

Welverdiend

Kalahari Game Lodge

Mata Mata

Prohibited entry or exit

49   C17

Wegdraai   D616   D579   D511   D603

20

14

Twee Rivier

24

D1119

75   C15

Bloukop

D1032   D1002

D1109

C18   48   Karaam

Haruchas   *War Memorials 1905*

Grauwater   72

C15

Persip

Bulwana

36

29

D617   D620

D1065   Dooisvlei   35

Leybank

41

Oliifants

Auob

Eindpaal

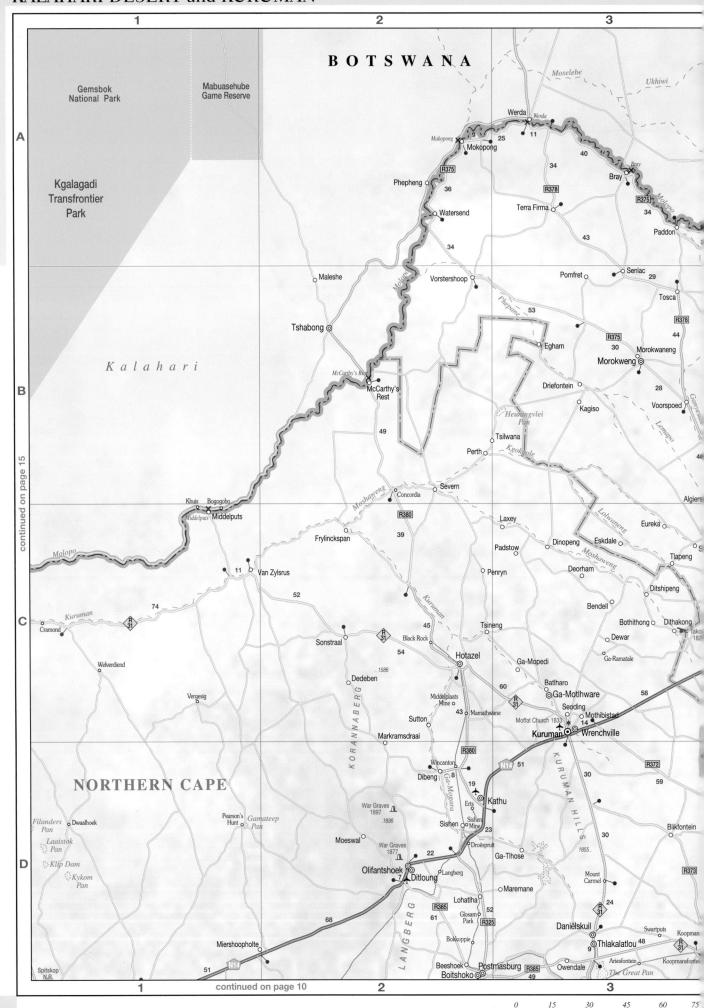

BOTSWANA

Gemsbok National Park

Mabuasehube Game Reserve

Kgalagadi Transfrontier Park

Moselebe

Ukhiwi

Werda

Makopong 9

25

11

Mokopong

40

34

R375

Bray

Phepheng 36

R378

34

Molopo

Watersend

Terra Firma

R375

Paddon

34

34

K a l a h a r i

Maleshe

Vorstershoop

Pomfret

Senlac 29

Tosca

Phepane

53

R378

Tshabong

Egham

30

R375

44

Morokwaneng

Morokweng

McCarthy's Rest

McCarthy's Rest

Driefontein

28

Voorspoed

Heuningvlei Pan

Kagiso

Lemapo

49

Tsilwana

Gianyesou

Perth

Kgokgole

Algiers

continued on page 15

Severn

Concordia

Moshaweng

R380

Laxey

Lohwaneng

Eureka

Khuis Bogogobo

Middelputs Middelputs

39

Dinopeng

Eskdale

Padstow

Moshaweng

Tlapeng

Frylinckspan

Molopo

Deorham

Penryn

11 Van Zylsrus

52

Kuruman

Ditshipeng

74

R31

Kuruman

Bendell

45

Tsineng

Bothithong

Dithakong

Cramond

Black Rock

Dewar

Tako

182

Sonstraal

R31

Hotazel

Ga-Mopedi

Ga-Ramatale

54

.1586

Welverdiend

Batlharo

58

Dedeben

60

Ga-Motlhware

Middelplaats Mine

Seoding

Vergesig

43 Mamathwane

14 Mothibistad

Sutton

Moffat Church 1833

K O R A N N A B E R G

Markramsdraai

Kuruman Wrenchville

NORTHERN CAPE

Wincanton

R380

N14 51

R372

Dibeng 8

30

59

Ga-Mogara

19

Filanders Pan

Dwaalhoek

Pearson's Hunt

Gamateep Pan

War Graves 1897

.1836

Erts

Kathu

K U R U M A N   H I L L S

Blikfontein

Sishen

Sishen Mine

23

30

Laaistok Pan

Moeswal

War Graves 1877

Droëspruit

Ga-Tlhose

1855.

Mount Carmel

R373

Klip Dam

22

Olifantshoek

Ditloung

Langberg

Maremane

24

R31

Kykom Pan

7

Lohatlha

R385

52

Daniëlskuil

Swartputs

Koopman

Glosam Park

61

R325

Thlakalatlou 48

R31

Spitskop N.R.

Miershoopholte

L A N G B E R G

Bokkoppie

9

Ariesfontein

Koopmansfontei

Beeshoek

Postmasburg

R385

Owendale

The Great Pan

51 N14

Boitshoko

49

continued on page 10

0   15   30   45   60   75

continued on page 20

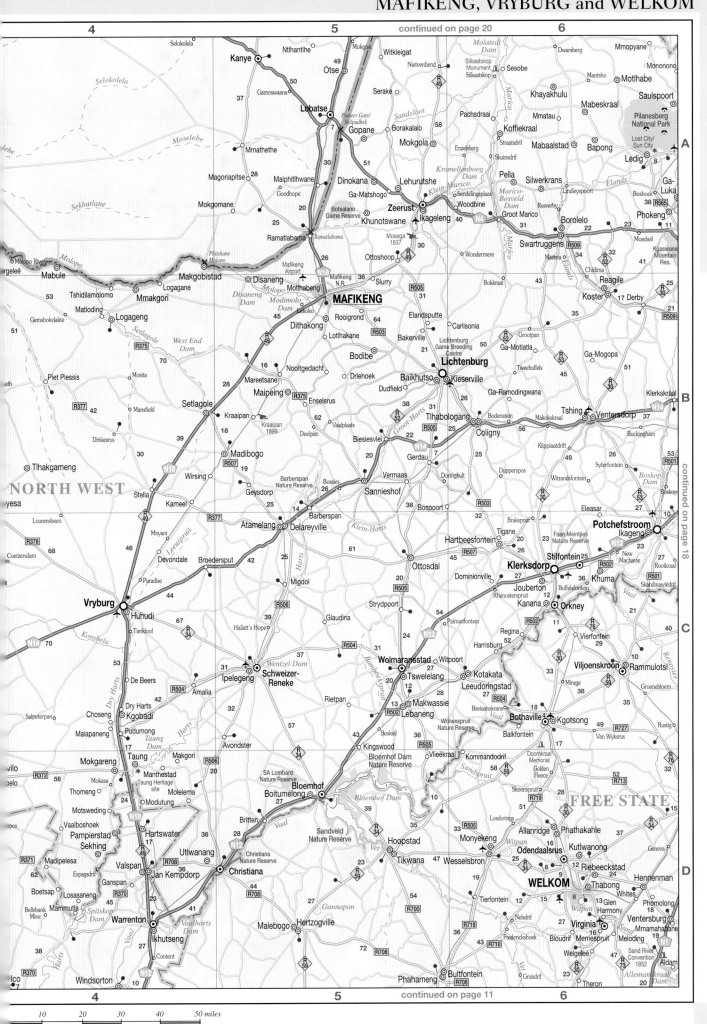

continued on page 11

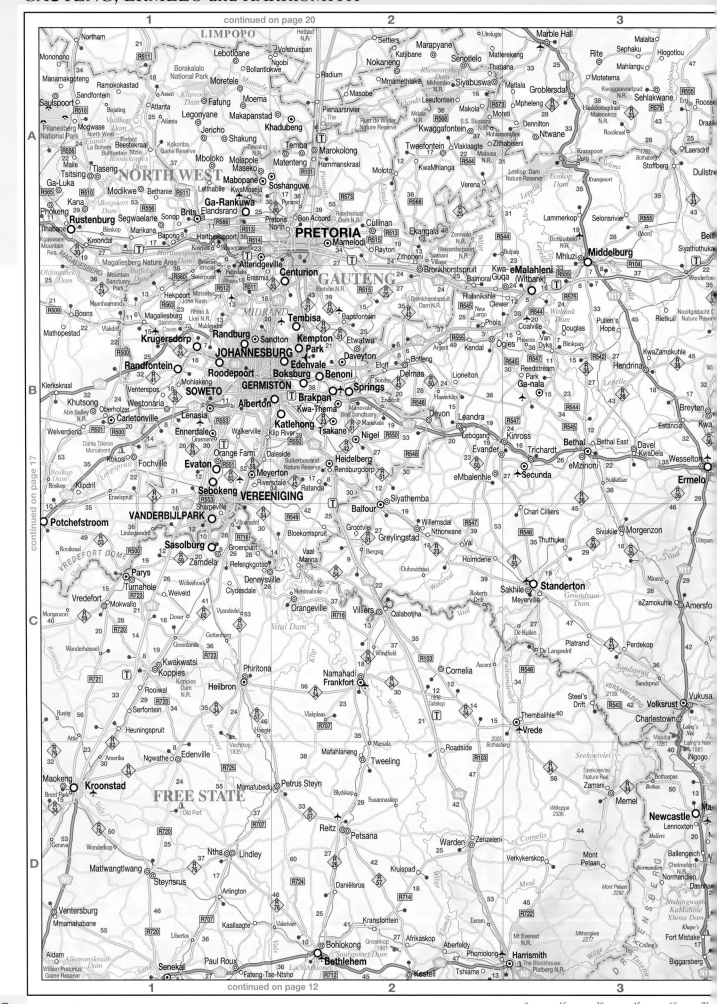

continued on page 20

continued on page 17

continued on page 12

0   15   30   45   60   75

continued on page 21

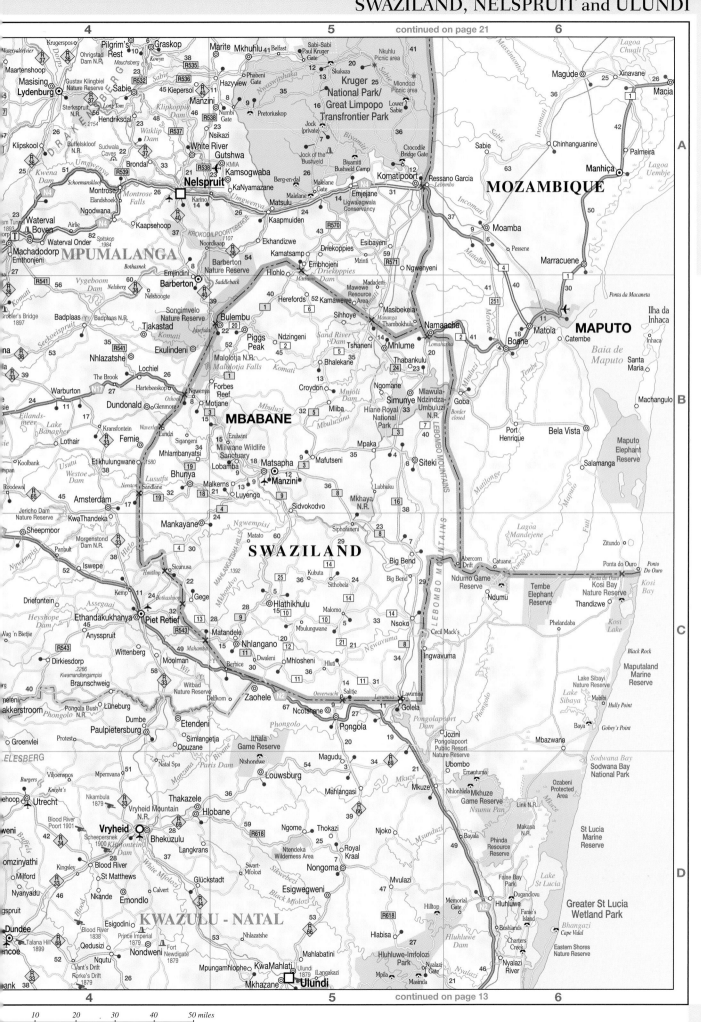

continued on page 13

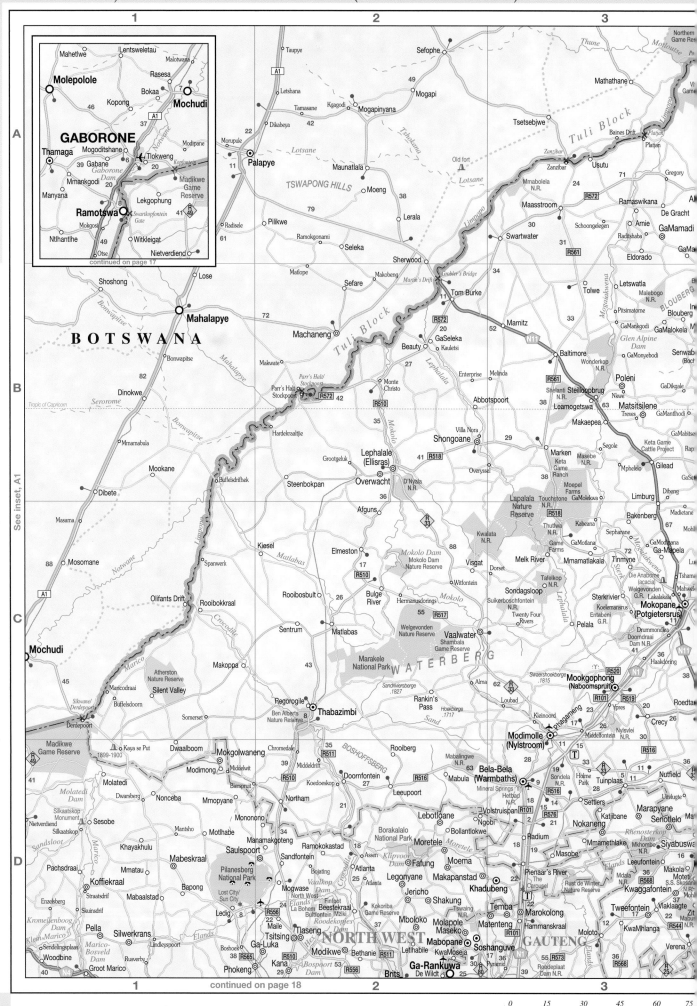

continued on page 17

continued on page 18

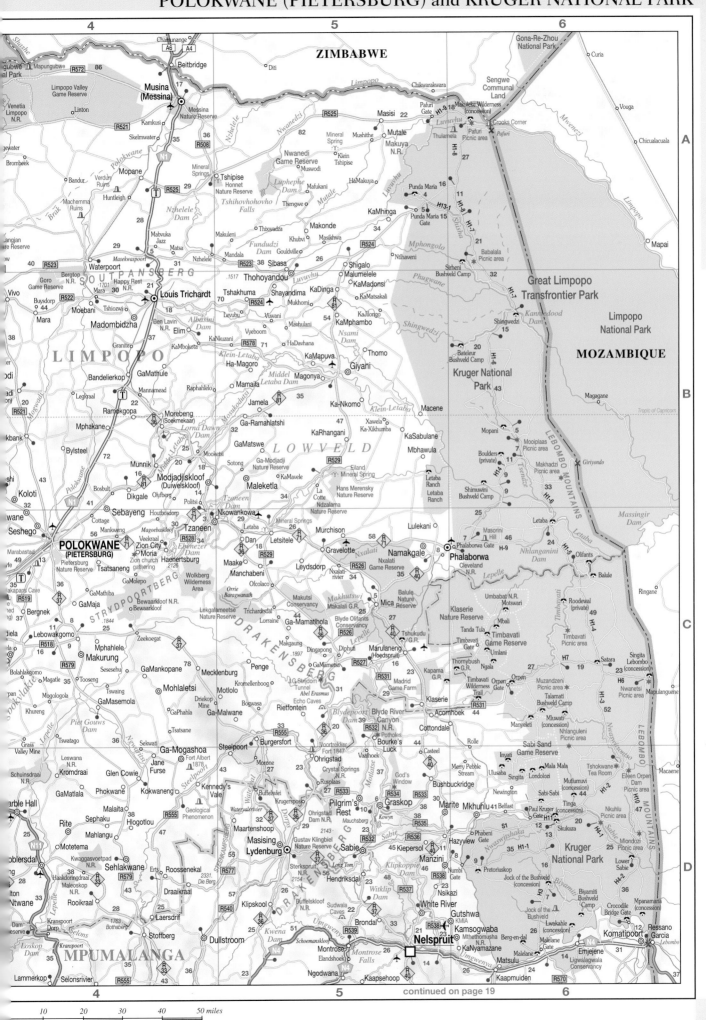

continued on page 19

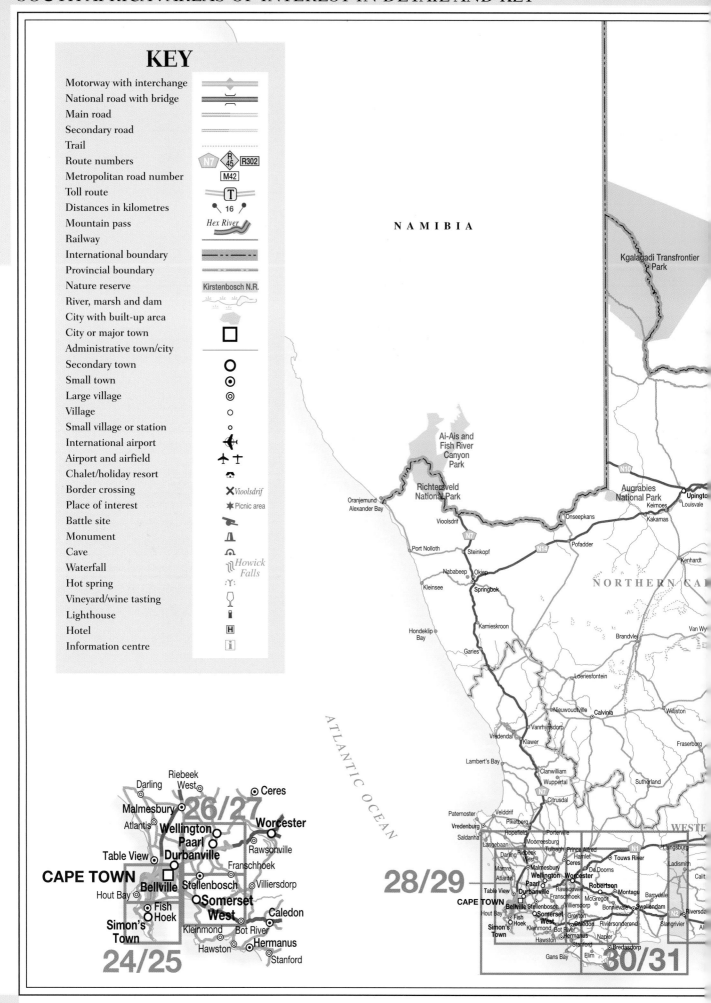

KEY

Motorway with interchange	
National road with bridge	
Main road	
Secondary road	
Trail	
Route numbers	N7 R45 R302
Metropolitan road number	M42
Toll route	T
Distances in kilometres	16
Mountain pass	Hex River
Railway	
International boundary	
Provincial boundary	
Nature reserve	Kirstenbosch N.R.
River, marsh and dam	
City with built-up area	
City or major town	▢
Administrative town/city	
Secondary town	○
Small town	◉
Large village	◎
Village	○
Small village or station	∘
International airport	✈
Airport and airfield	✈ ✈
Chalet/holiday resort	⌂
Border crossing	✗ Vioolsdrif
Place of interest	★ Picnic area
Battle site	
Monument	⊥
Cave	∩
Waterfall	Howick Falls
Hot spring	:Y:
Vineyard/wine tasting	⌾
Lighthouse	
Hotel	H
Information centre	ℹ

NAMIBIA

Kgalagadi Transfrontier Park

Ai-Ais and Fish River Canyon Park

Richtersveld National Park

Oranjemund
Alexander Bay

Augrabies National Park

Upington
Louisvale

Vioolsdrif

Keimoes
Onseepkans
Kakamas

Port Nolloth
Steinkopf
Pofadder

NORTHERN CA

Kenhardt

Nababeep Okiep
Springbok

Kleinsee

Hondeklip Bay
Kamieskroon

Brandvlei

Van Wy

Garies

Loeriesfontein

Nieuwoudtville Calvinia

Williston

Vredendal Vanrhynsdorp
Klawer

Fraserburg

Lambert's Bay

Clanwilliam
Wuppertal

Sutherland

Citrusdal

Paternoster Velddrif
Vredenburg Piketberg
Saldanha Hopefield Porterville

WESTE

Langebaan Moorreesburg
Darling Riebeek West Tulbagh Prince Alfred Hamlet
Mamre Malmesbury Ceres De Doorns
Atlantis Wellington Worcester

28/29 Table View Paarl Robertson Montagu Barrydale
Durbanville Franschhoek McGregor
CAPE TOWN Bellville Stellenbosch Villiersdorp Bonnievale Swellendam
Hout Bay Somerset Greyton Riviersonderend
Simon's Fish West Caledon
Town Hoek Bot River Napier
Hawston Stanford Elim
Hermanus Bredasdorp
Gans Bay

ATLANTIC OCEAN

Riebeek West
Darling Ceres
Malmesbury 26/27
Atlantis Wellington Worcester
Paarl
Table View Durbanville Rawsonville
Franschhoek
CAPE TOWN Stellenbosch Villiersdorp
Bellville
Hout Bay Somerset West Caledon
Fish Hoek
Simon's Kleinmond Bot River
Town Hawston Hermanus
24/25 Stanford

30/31

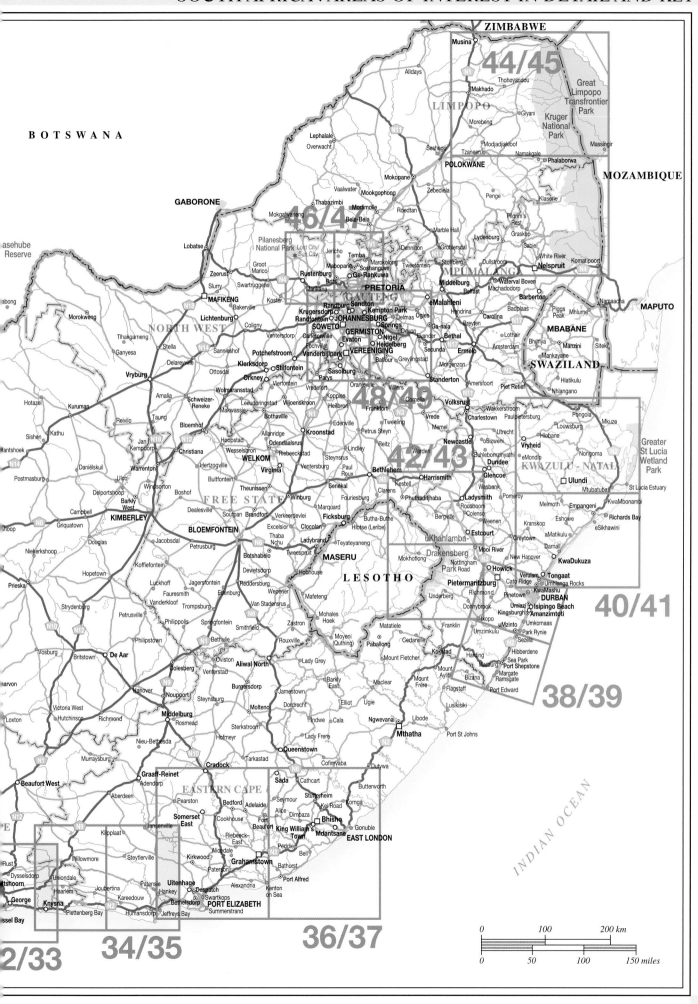

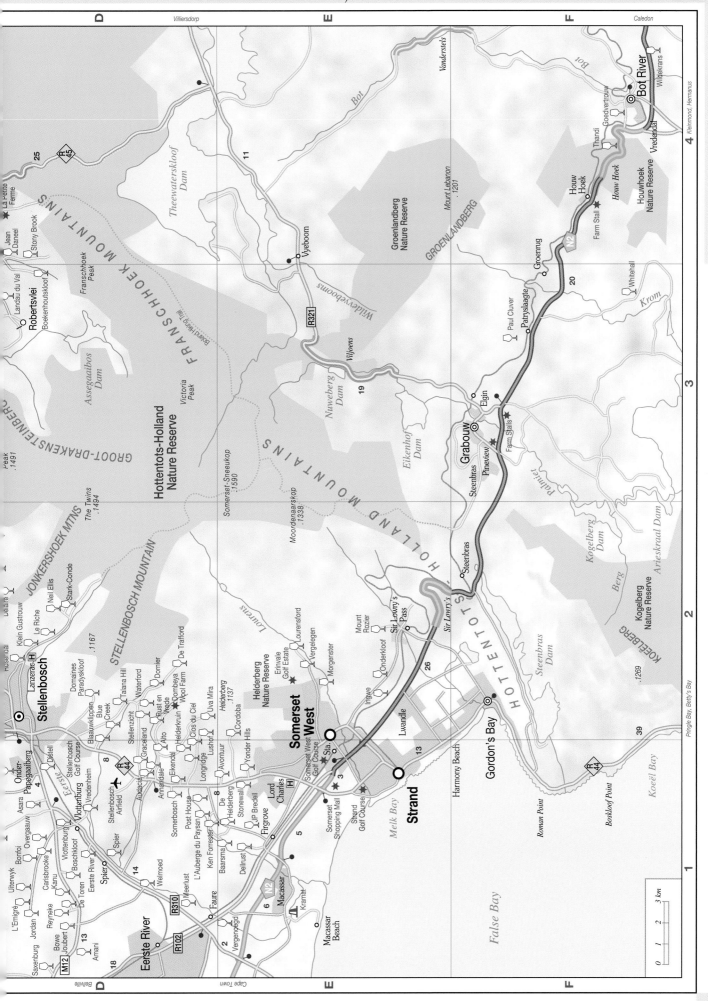

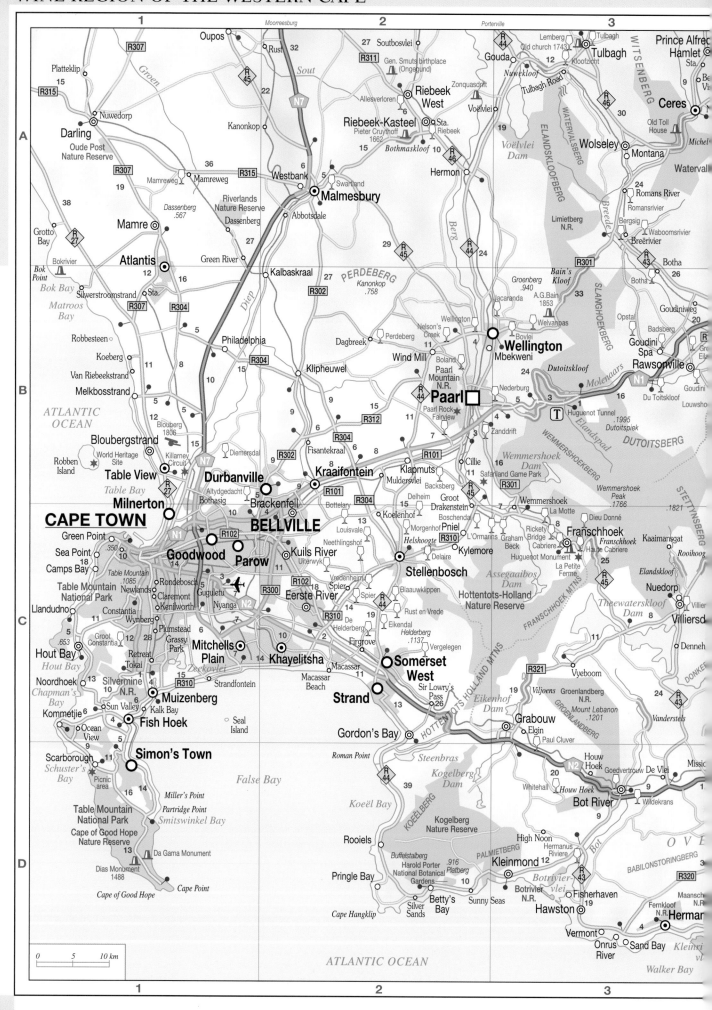

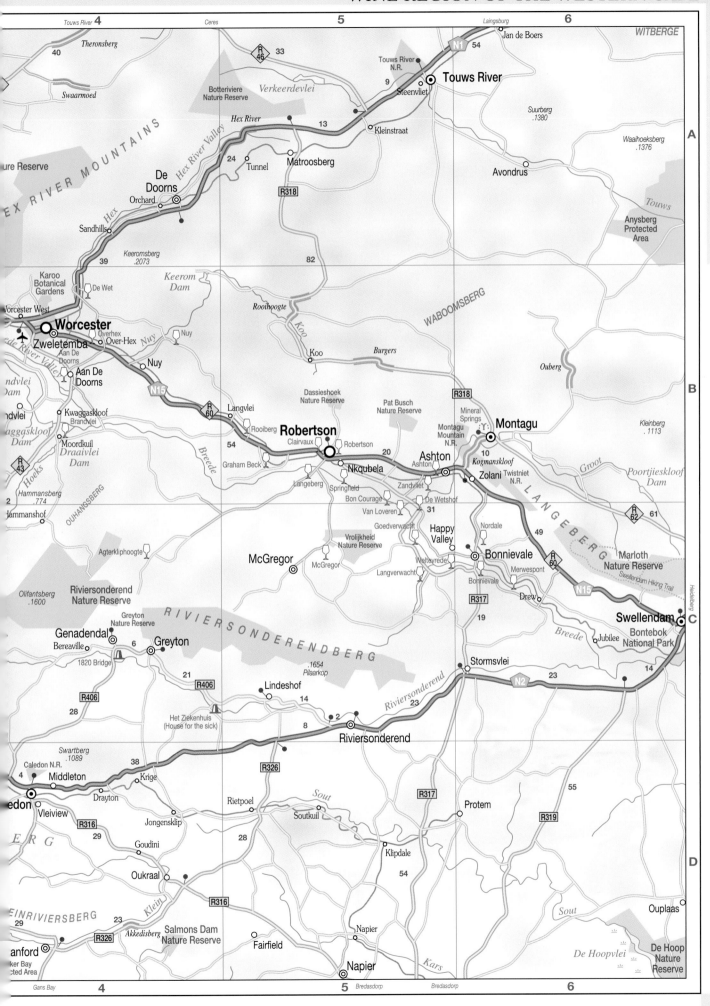

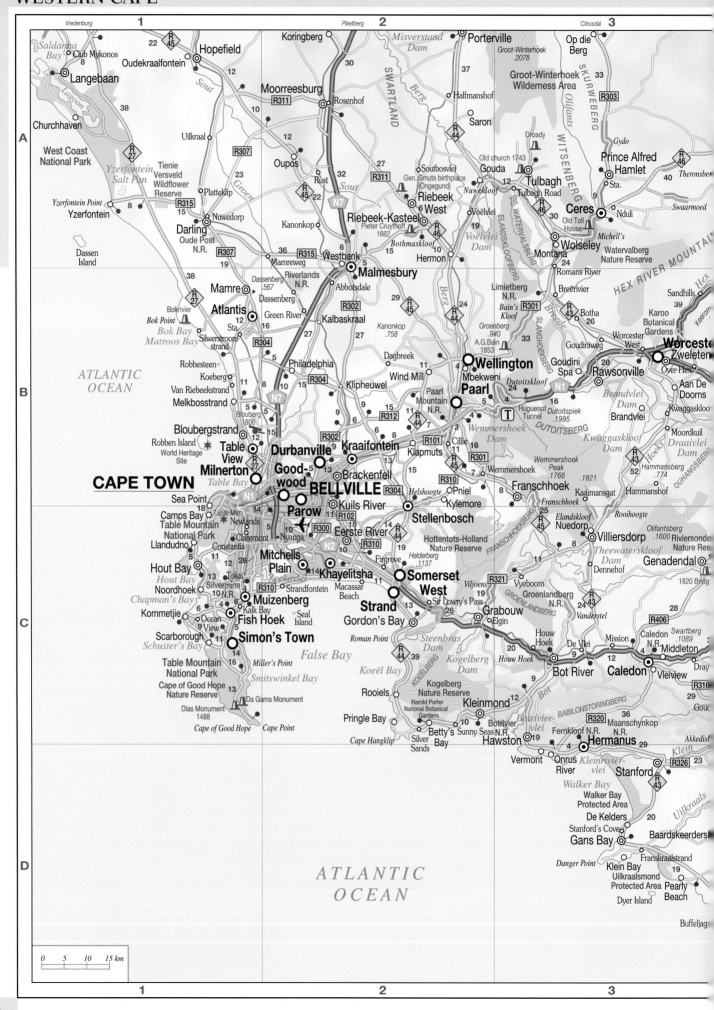

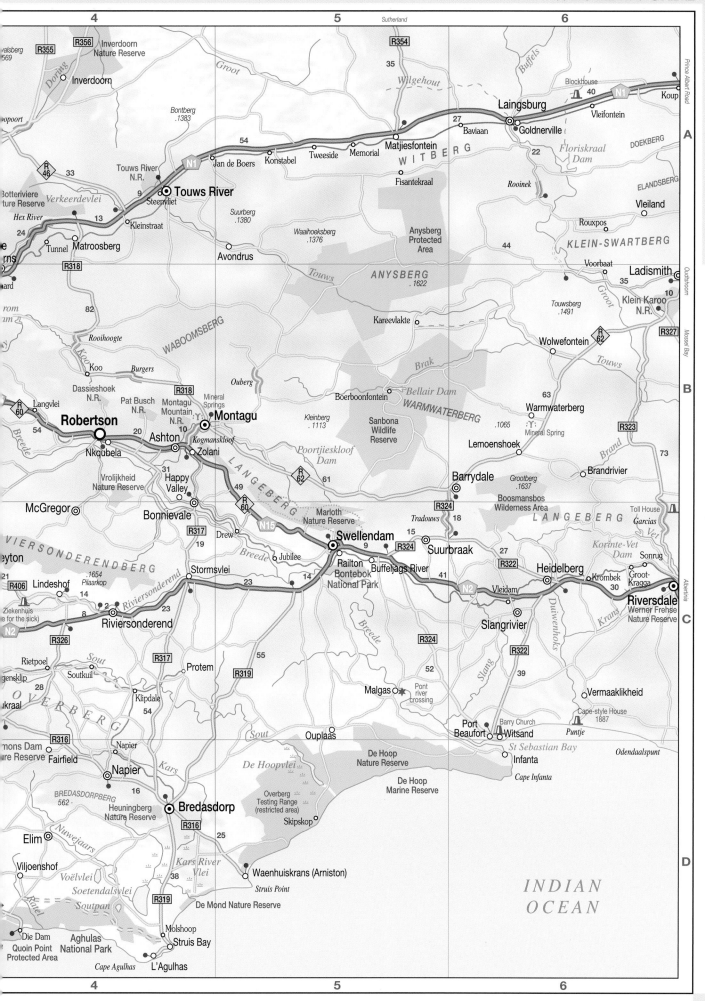

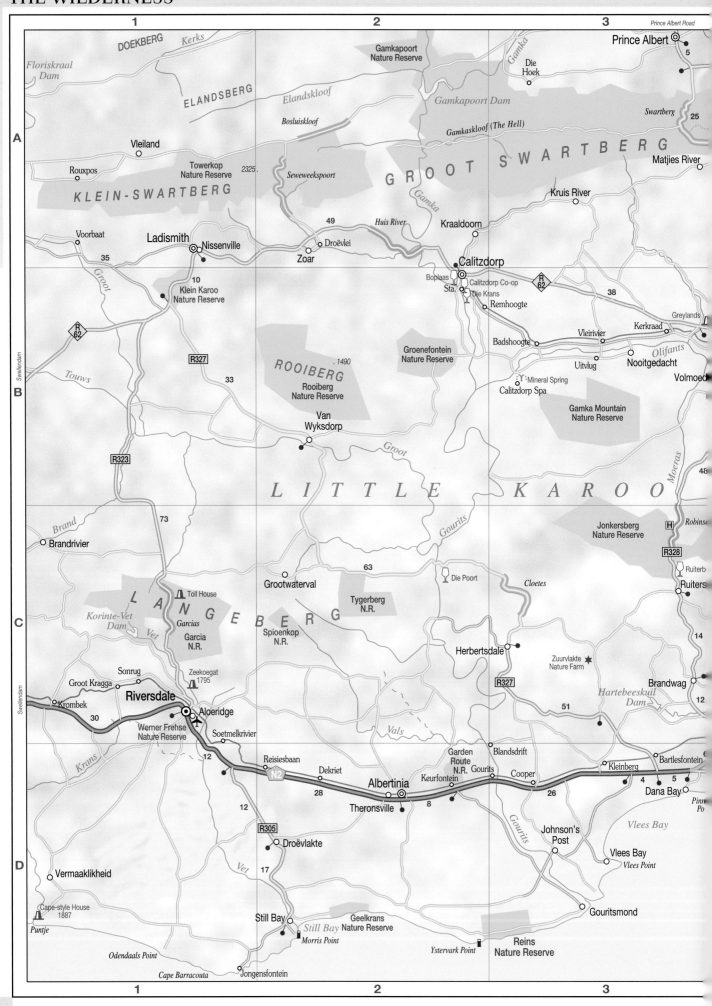

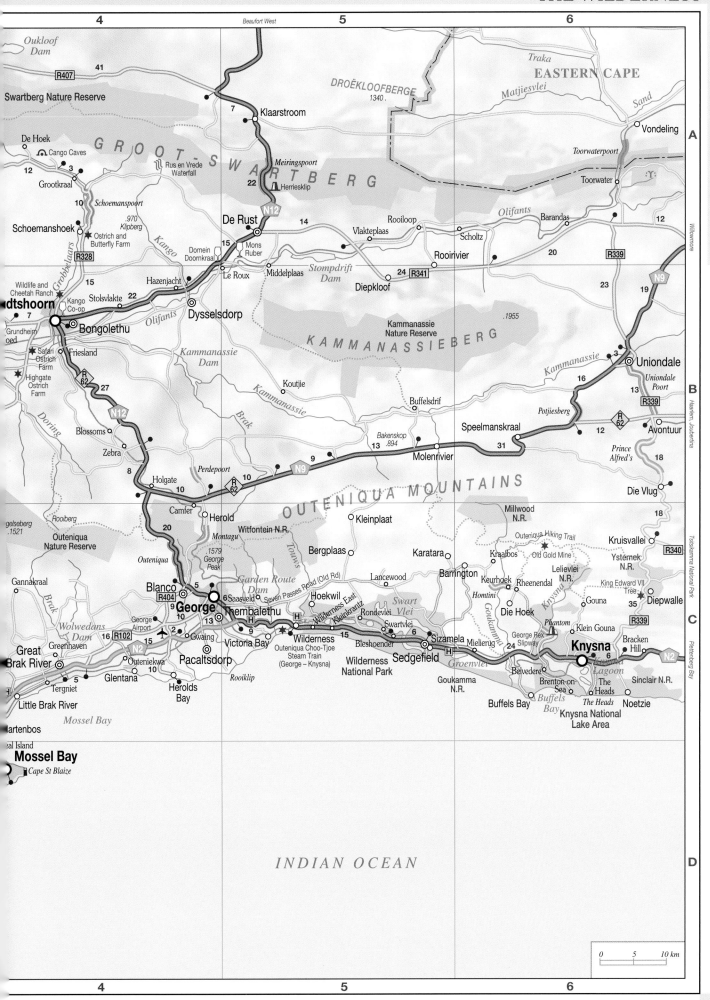

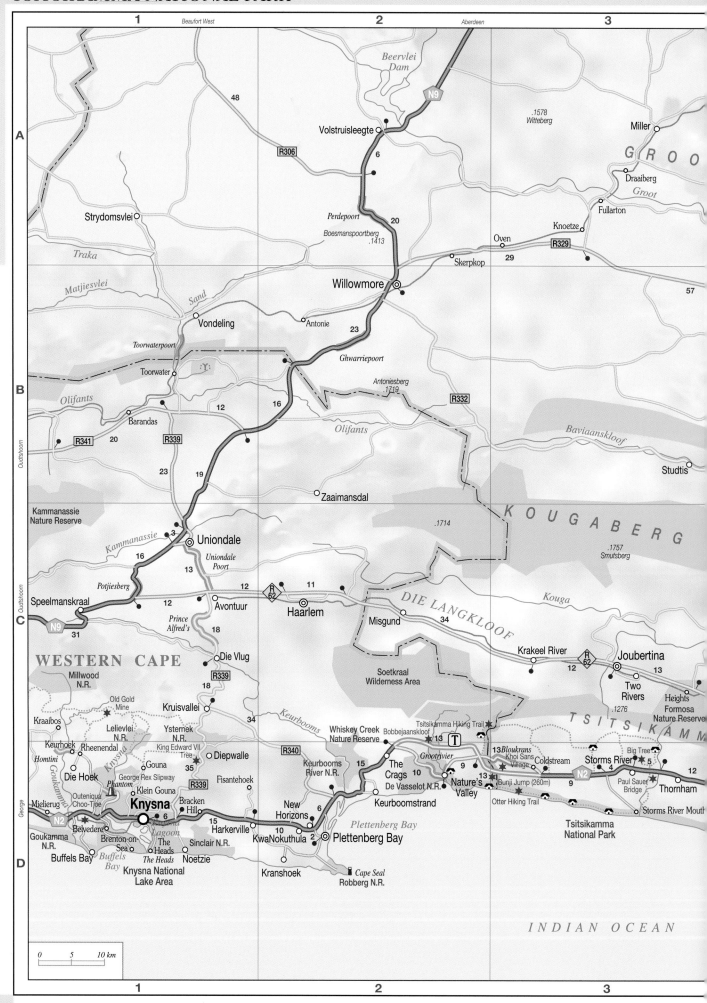

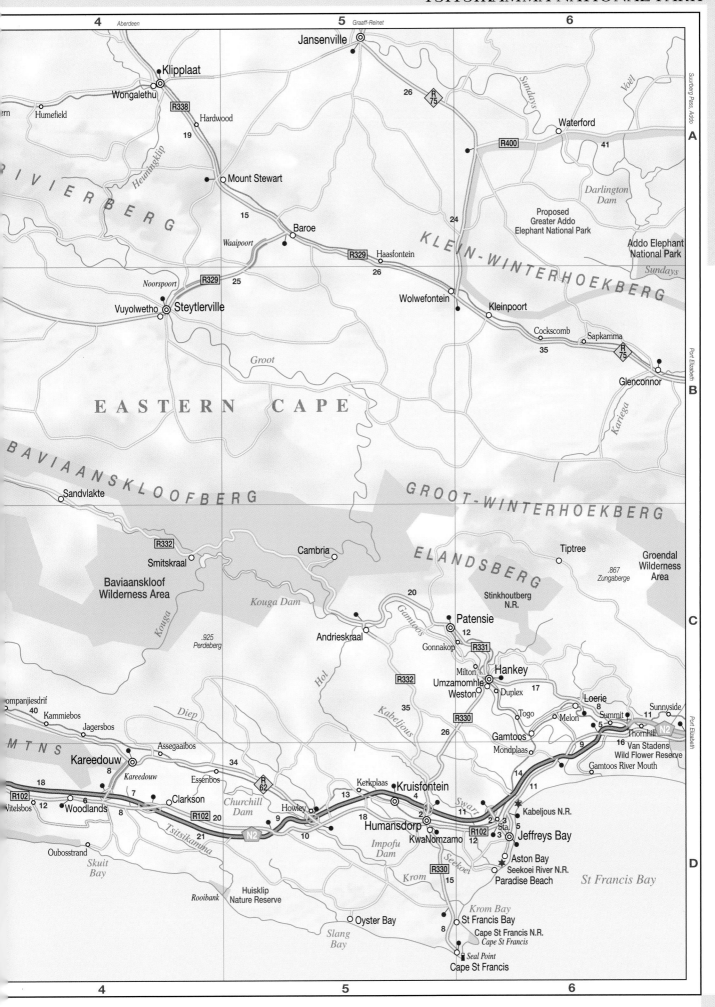

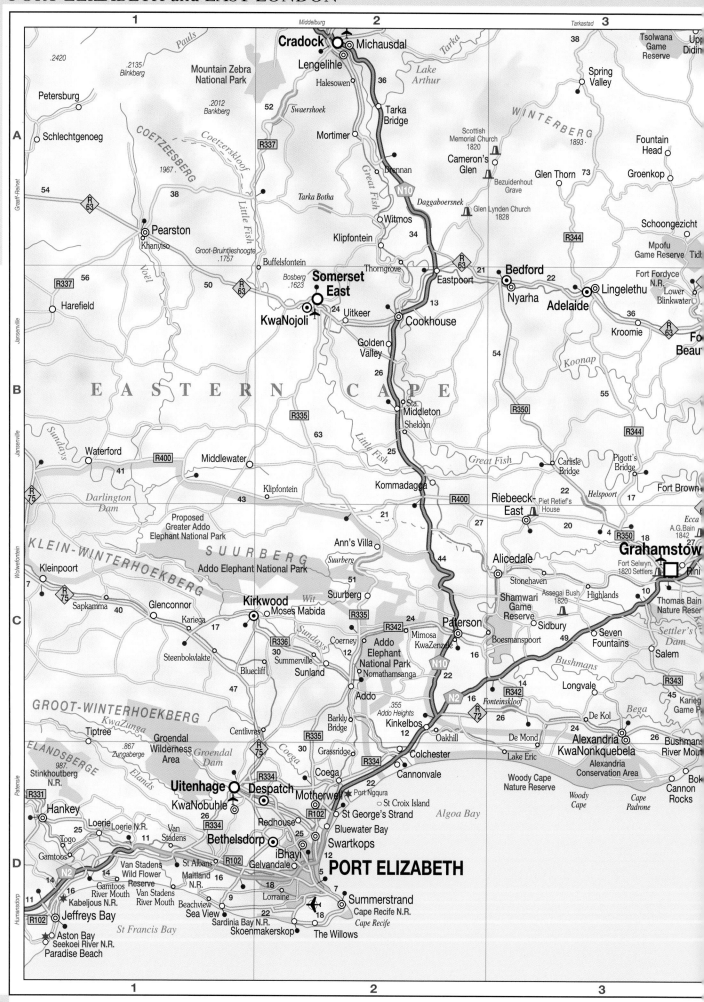

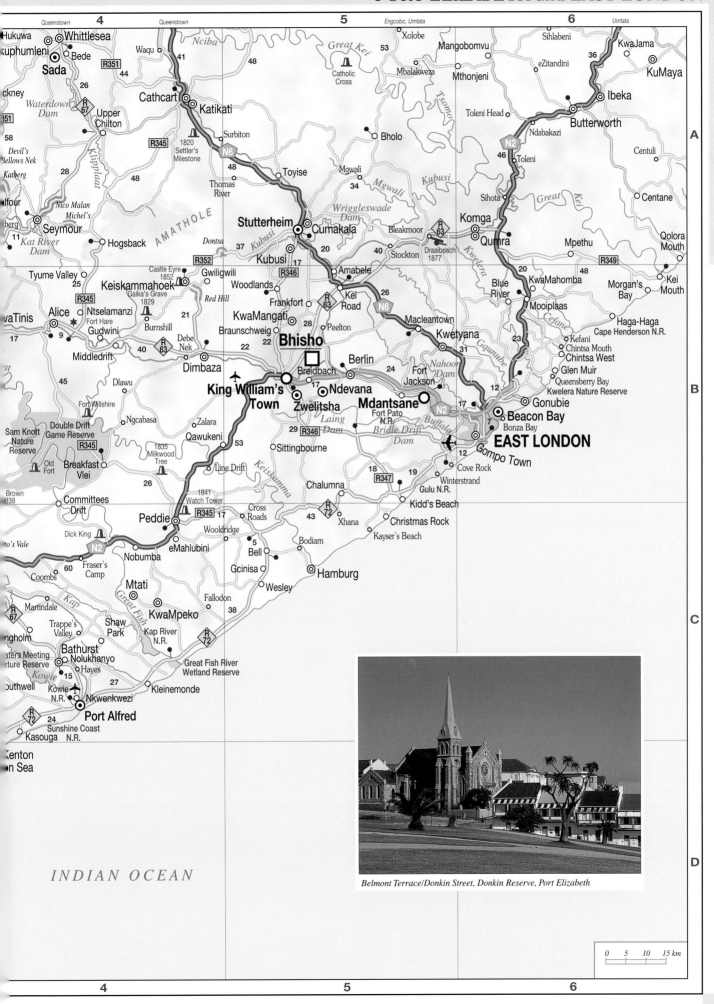

Belmont Terrace/Donkin Street, Donkin Reserve, Port Elizabeth

INDIAN OCEAN

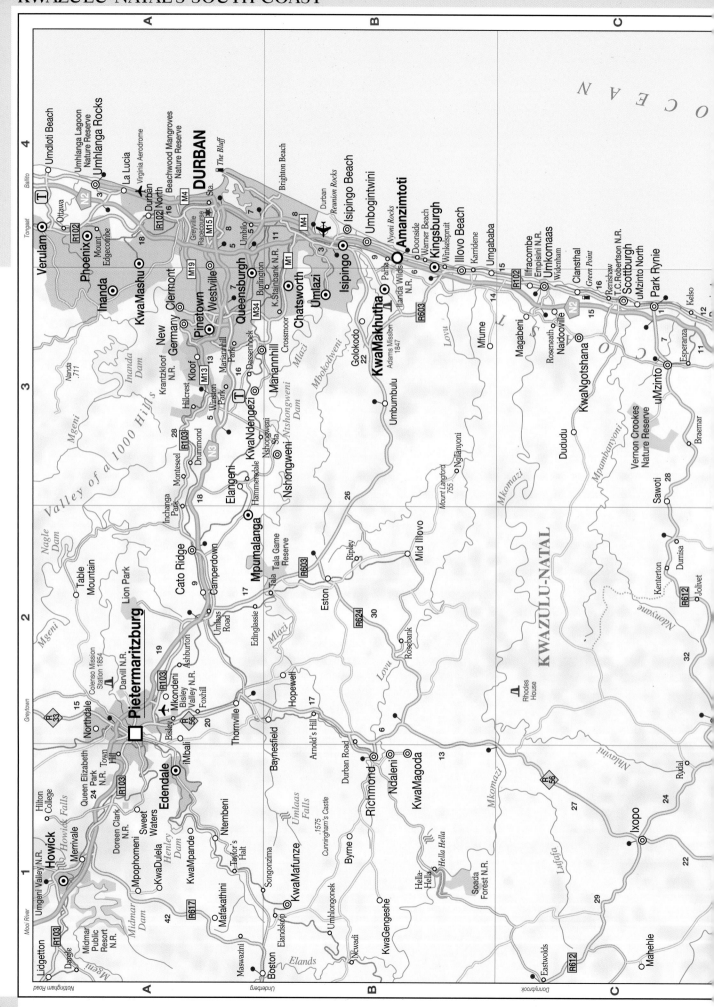

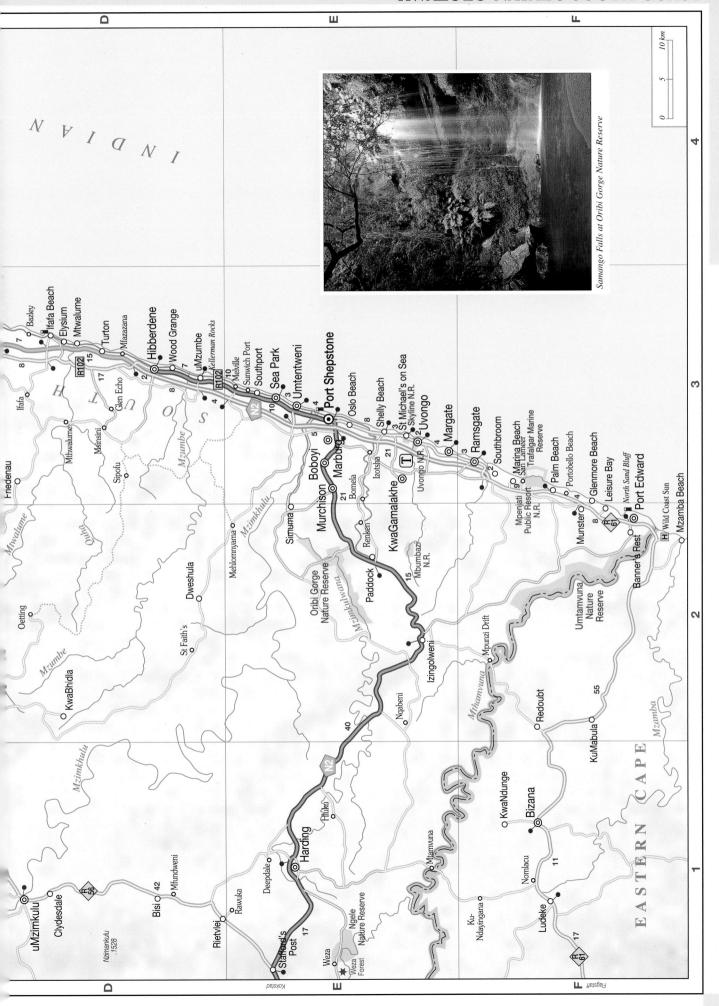

Samango Falls at Oribi Gorge Nature Reserve

10 km

5

0

I N D I A N

Bazley
Ifafa Beach
Elysium
Mtwalume
Turton
Mtezazana
Hibberdene
Wood Grange
uMzumbe
Kelleman Rocks
Melville
Sunwich Port
Southport
Sea Park
Umtentweni
Port Shepstone
Oslo Beach
Shelly Beach
St Michael's on Sea
Skyline N.R.
Uvongo
Margate
Ramsgate
Southbroom
Marina Beach
San Lameer
Trafalgar Marine Reserve
Palm Beach
Portobello Beach
Glenmore Beach
Leisure Bay
North Sand Bluff
Port Edward
Mzamba Beach
Wild Coast Sun

Ifafa
Glen Echo
Msinsini
R102
R102
N2

Friedenau
Mthwalume
Sipofu
Oetting
KwaBhidla
Mzumbe
Ouha
Mwalume
Mzimkhulu

Boboyi
Murchison
Marburg
KwaGamalakhe
Bomela
Renken
Izotsha
Izingolweni
Simuna
Mehlomnyama
Dweshula
St Faith's

Oribi Gorge Nature Reserve
Mzimkulwana
Paddock
Mbumbazi N.R.
Uvongo N.R.
Mpenjati Public Resort N.R.
Munstero
Banner's Rest

Umtamvuna Nature Reserve
Mthamvuna
Mpunzi Drift
Ngabeni

Redoubt
KuMabula
Mzamba

KwaNdunge
Bizana
Mtamvuna

uMzimkulu
Clydesdale
Nzimankulu .1528
Bisi
Mfundweni
Rietvlei
Deepdale
Harding
Hluku
Rawuka
Stafford's Post
Weza
Weza Forest
Ngele Nature Reserve

Ku-Ndayingana
Nomlacu
Ludeke

EASTERN CAPE

R 56
R 61
R 61

T
H
U
L
S
I
N
I

7
8
15
17
2
8
4
10
3
4
5
21
10
3
8
3
21
2
4
3
2
9
4
8
15
40
17
42
55
11
17
56

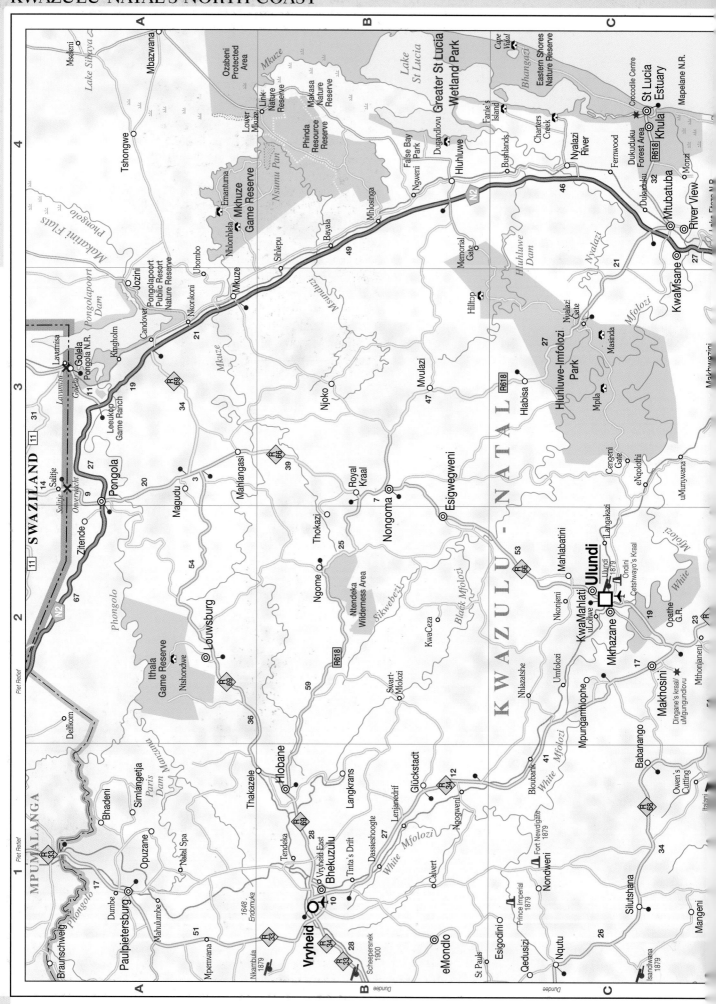

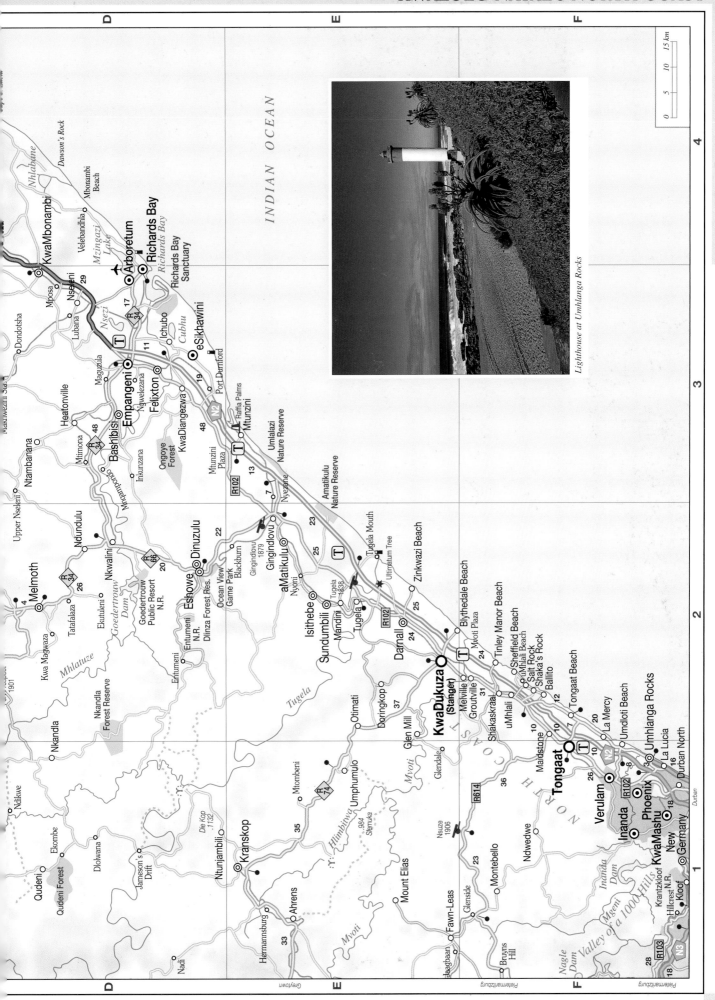

Lighthouse at Umhlanga Rocks

INDIAN OCEAN

Nhlabane
Dawson's Rock
Mbonambi Beach
KwaMbonambi
Velebandhla
Mzingazi Lake
Mposa
Nseleni
Lubana
Dondotsha
29
17
R 34
Arboretum
Richards Bay
Richards Bay
Richards Bay Sanctuary
Nsezi
Ichubo
Cubhu
eSikhawini
Maguzula
T
11
Heatonville
Empangeni
Felixton
Port Durnford
19
KwaDiangezwa
Ngwelezana
Ntambanana
Mtimona
48
R 34
Bashibisi
Inkunzana
48
Ongoye Forest
Rafia Palms
Mtunzini
N2
Upper Nseleni
Ndundulu
Nkwalini
Goedertrouw Dam
Mthebanduna
Mtunzini Plaza
T
Umlalazi
Nature Reserve
Mtunzini Nature Reserve
Ekutuleni
R 66
20
Goedertrouw Public Resort N.R.
R102
13
7
Nyezane
Amatikulu Nature Reserve
Melmoth
R 34
26
Nkwalini
Eshowe
Dinuzulu
22
Ocean View Game Park
Blackburn
Gingindlovu 1879
aMatikulu
25
23
Tugela Mouth
Ultimatum Tree
Zinkwazi Beach
4
Tatafalaza
Kwa Magwaza
Entumeni N.R.
Dlinza Forest Res.
Entumeni
Gingindlovu
Nyoni
T
Nkandla
Nkandla Forest Reserve
1901
Mhlatuze
Entumeni
Isithebe
Sundumbili
Mandini
Tugela 1838
Tugela
R102
25
Blythedale Beach
Myoti Plaza
Ndikwe
Nkandla
Darnall
24
Tinley Manor Beach
Sheffield Beach
uMhlali Beach
Salt Rock
Shaka's Rock
Ballito
Tugela
KwaDukuza (Stanger)
T
24
Qudeni
Ekombe
Dlolwana
Jameson's Drift
Die Kop .1732
Ntunjambili
Kranskop
Mtombeni
Mthunwa Umphumulo
984 Sifemuka
Glendale
Otimati
Doringkop
37
Glen Mill
Melville
Groutville
Shakaskraal
31
uMhlali
12
Tongaat Beach
Nadi
Ahrens
35
R 74
Mount Elias
Nsuze 1906
Montebello
23
Ndwedwe
Maidstone
10
10
La Mercy
Umdloti Beach
20
Umhlanga Rocks
La Lucia
Durban North
Hermannsburg
33
Fawn-Leas
Glenside
R614
36
Tongaat
26
N2
Verulam
R102
Phoenix
18
Inanda
KwaMashu
New Germany
Bruyns Hill
Nagle Dam
Mgeni
Valley of a 1000 Hills
Inanda Dam
Krantzkloof N.R.
Hillcrest N.R.
Kloof
R103
28
18
N3

NORTH COAST

0 5 10 15 km

41

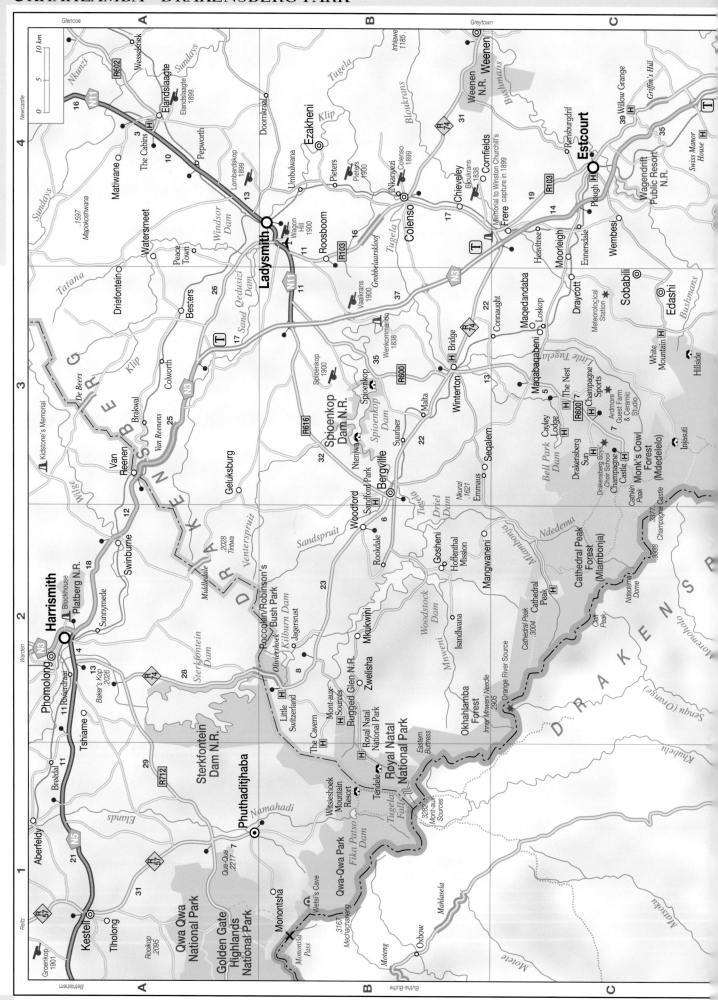

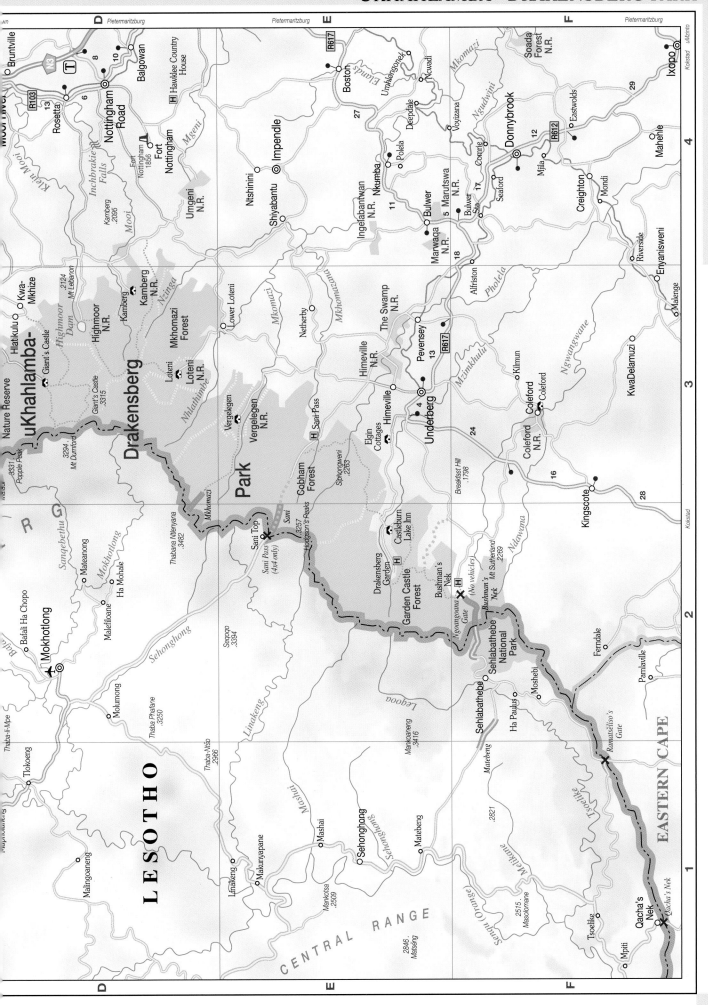

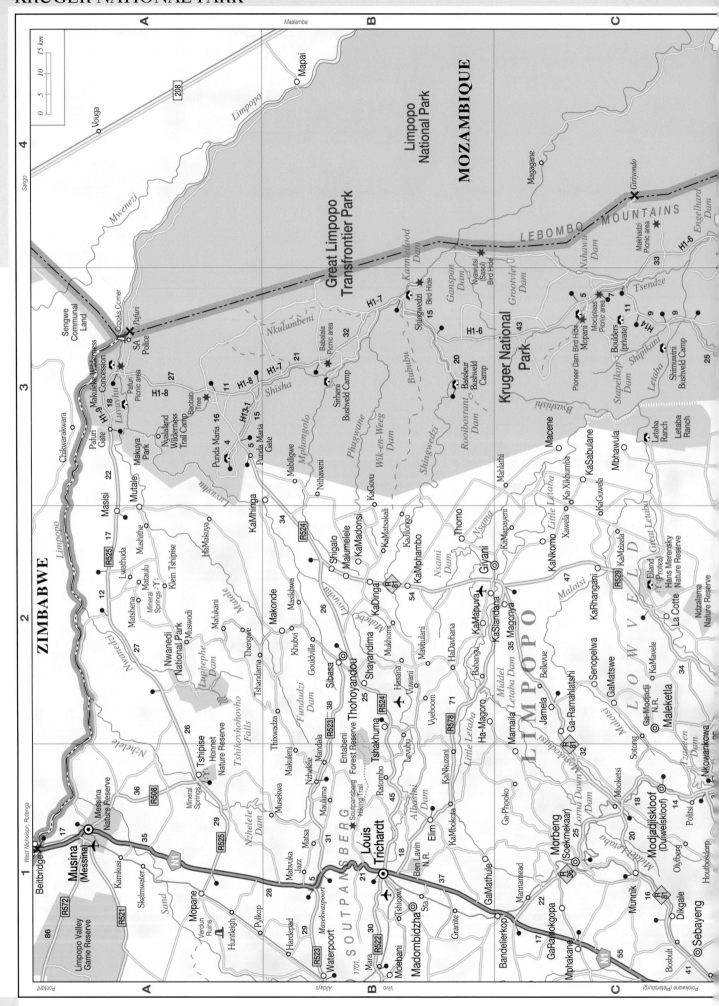

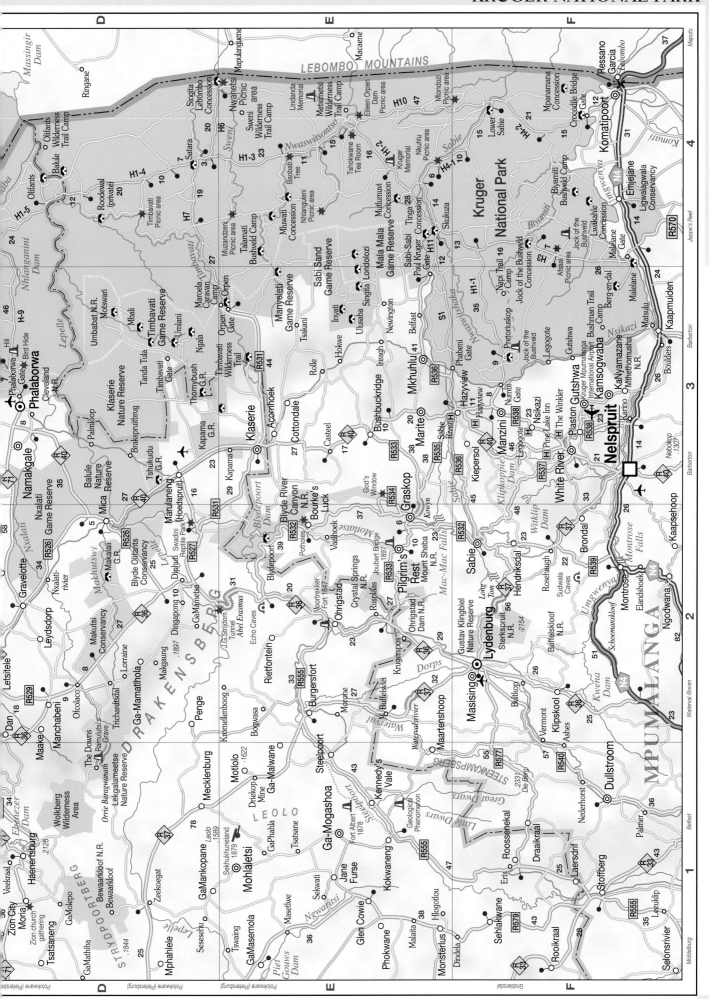

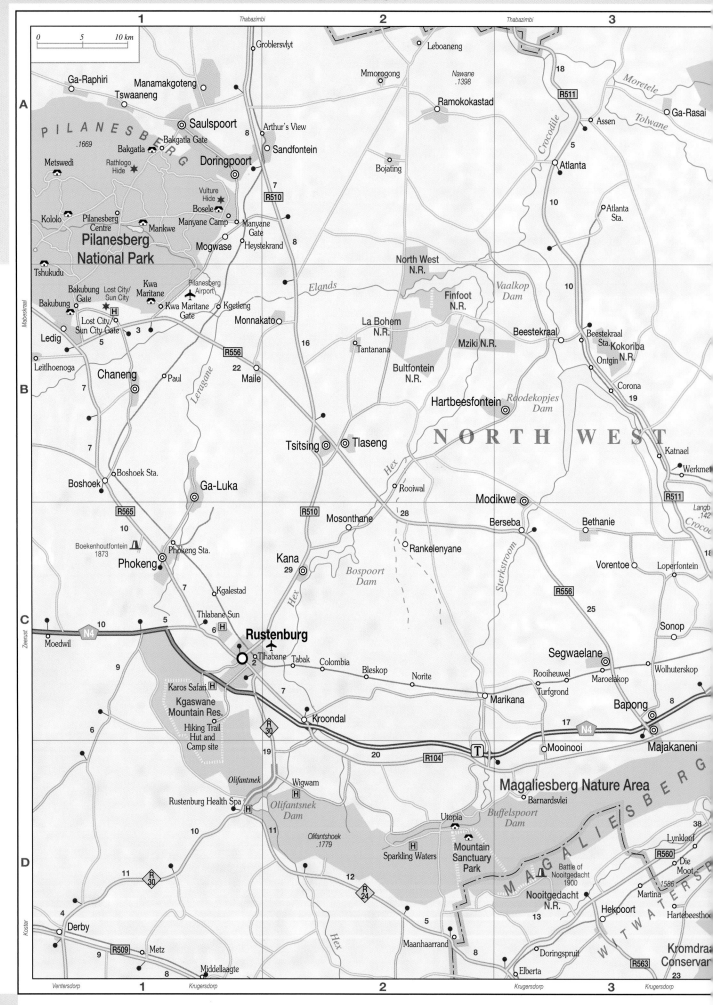

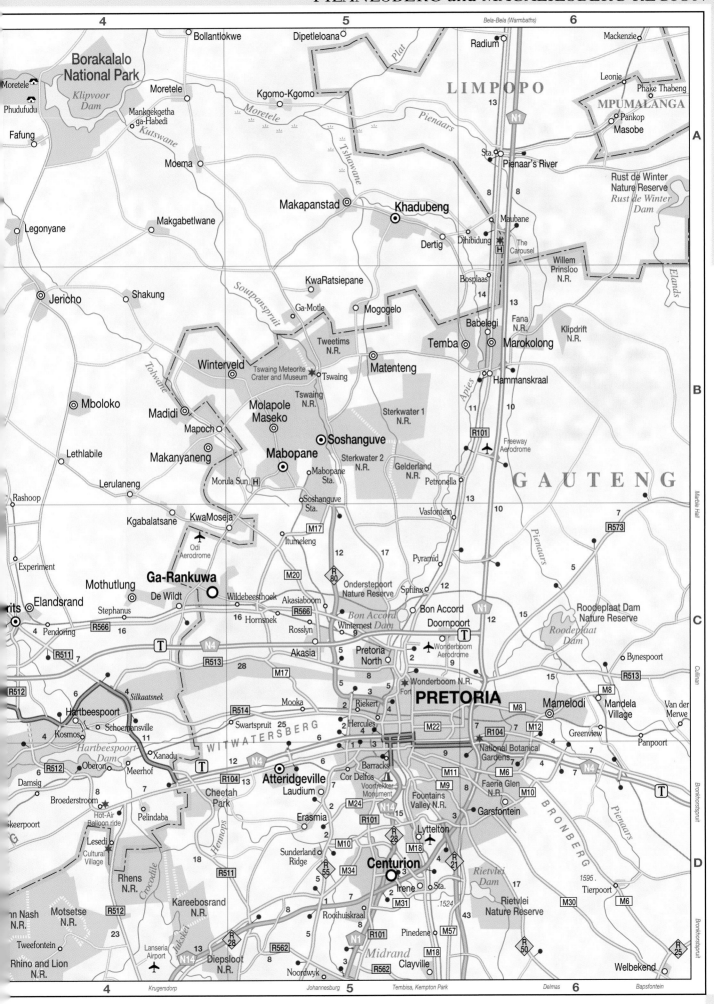

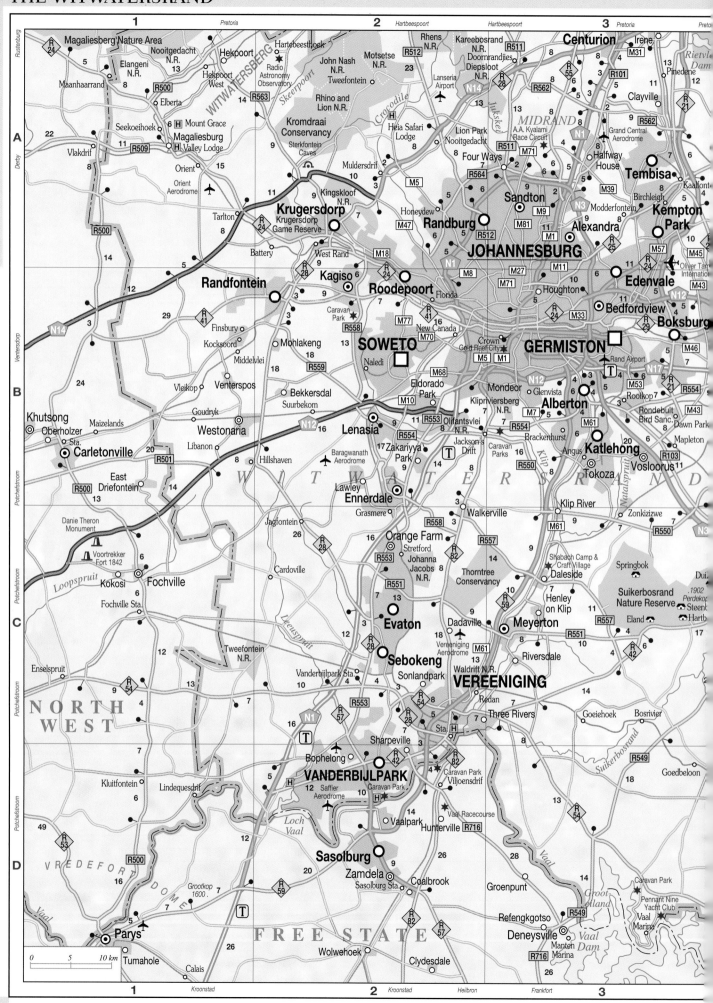

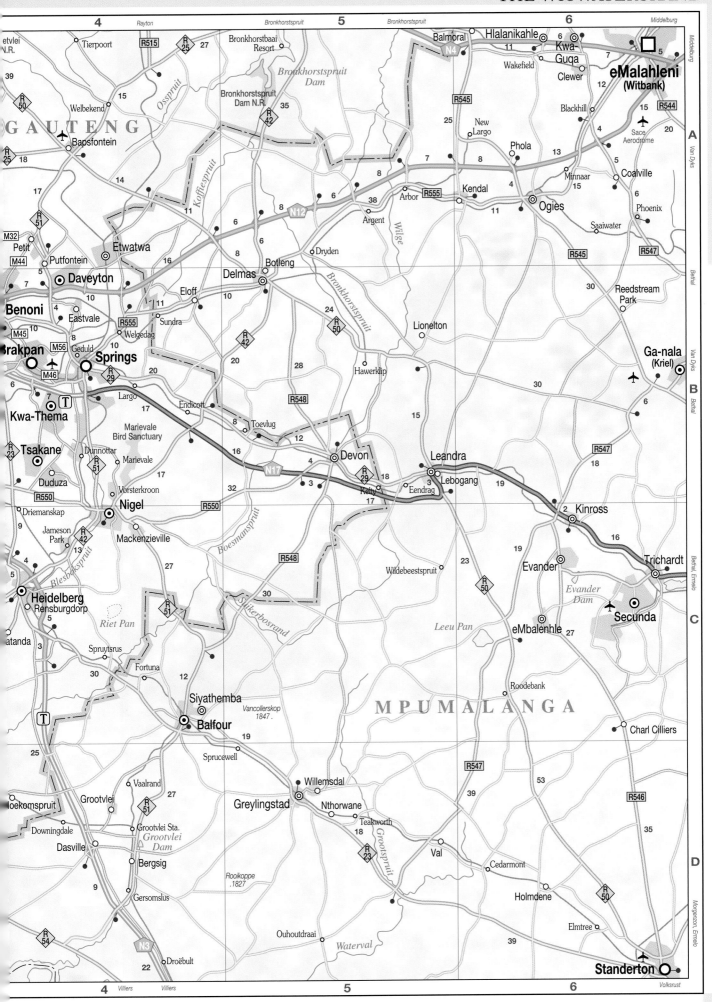

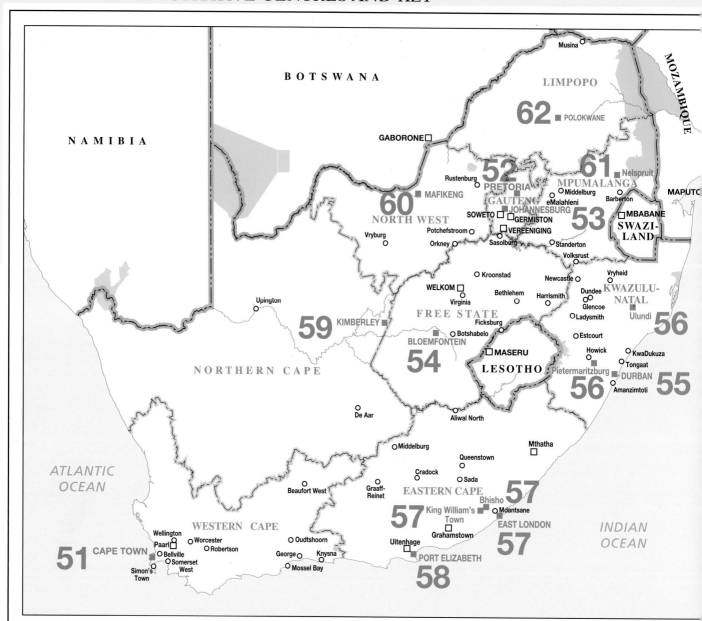

KEY

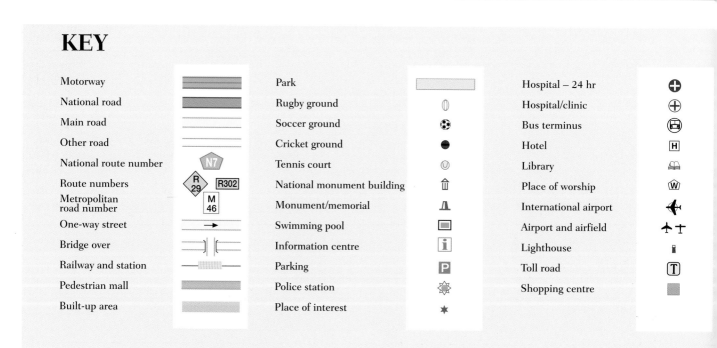

Motorway		Park		Hospital – 24 hr
National road		Rugby ground		Hospital/clinic
Main road		Soccer ground		Bus terminus
Other road		Cricket ground		Hotel
National route number	N7	Tennis court		Library
Route numbers	R29 R302	National monument building		Place of worship
Metropolitan road number	M46	Monument/memorial		International airport
One-way street	→	Swimming pool		Airport and airfield
Bridge over		Information centre		Lighthouse
Railway and station		Parking	P	Toll road
Pedestrian mall		Police station		Shopping centre
Built-up area		Place of interest		

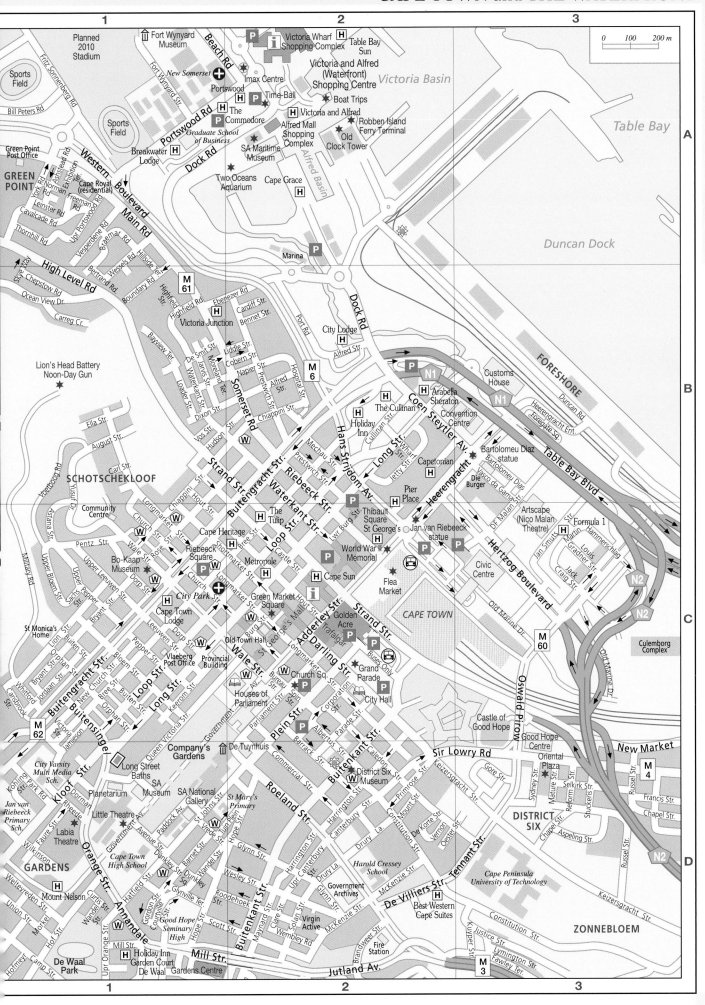

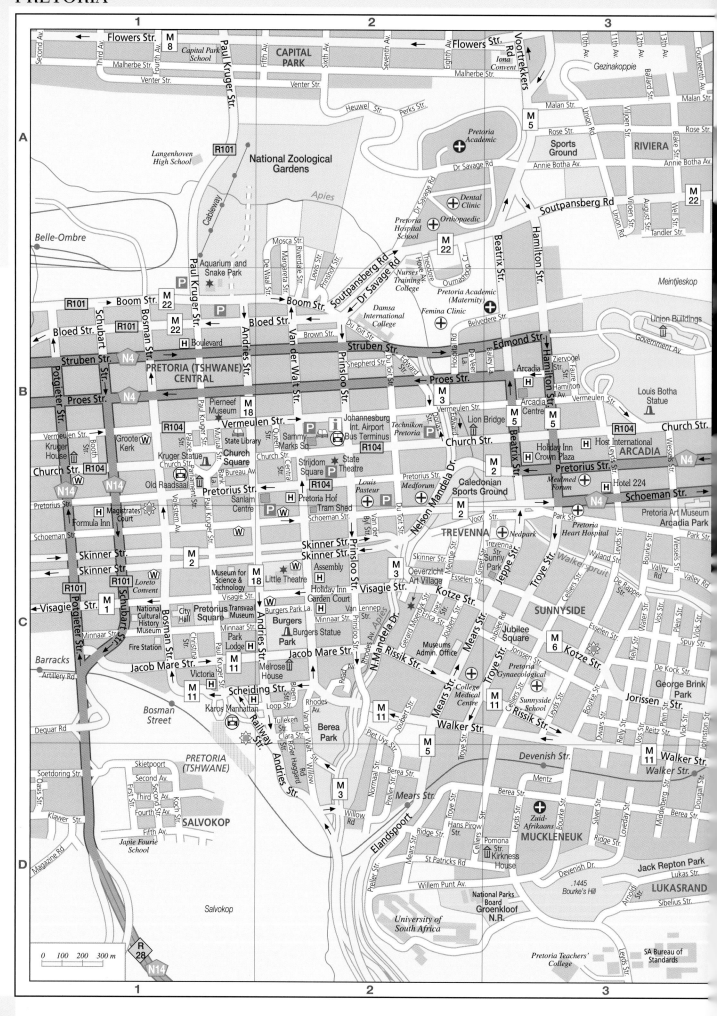

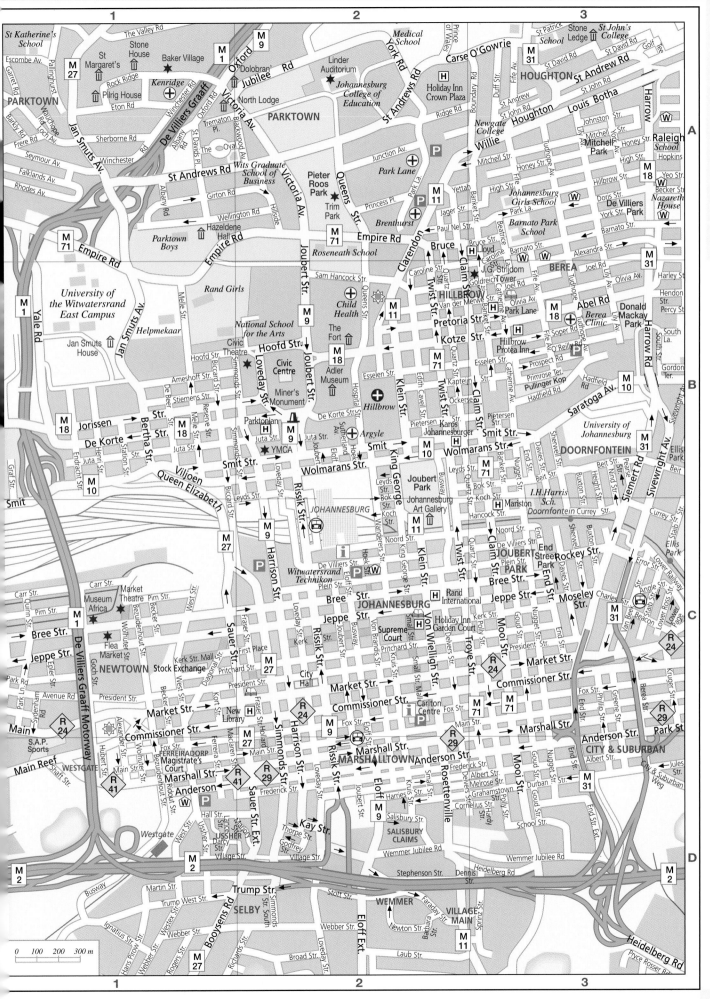

BLOEMFONTEIN and ENVIRONS

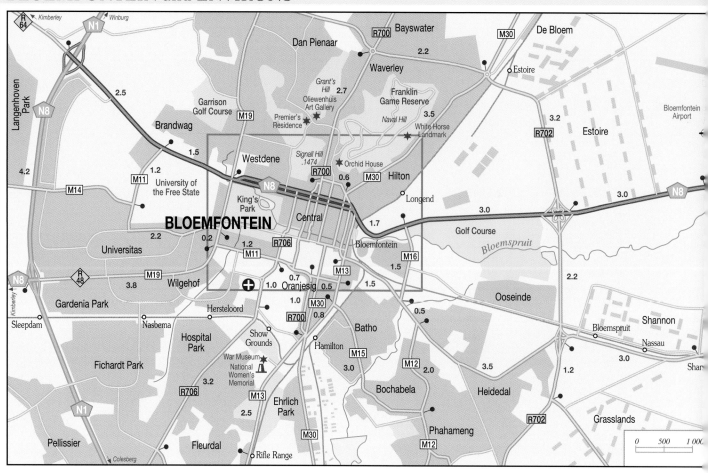

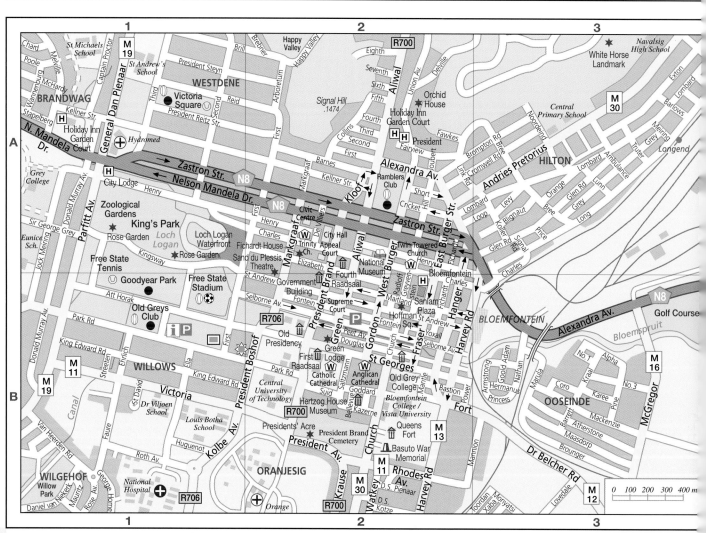

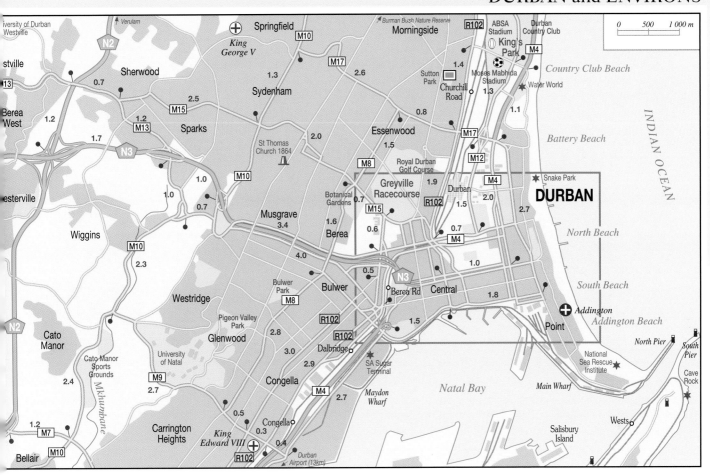

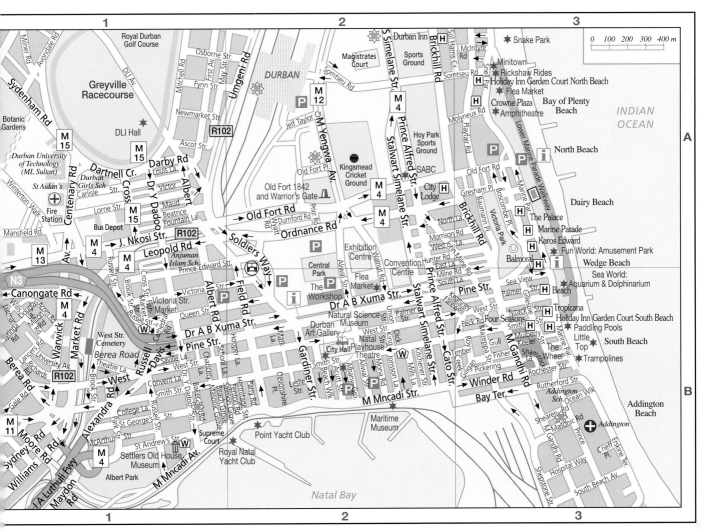

PIETERMARITZBURG and ULUNDI

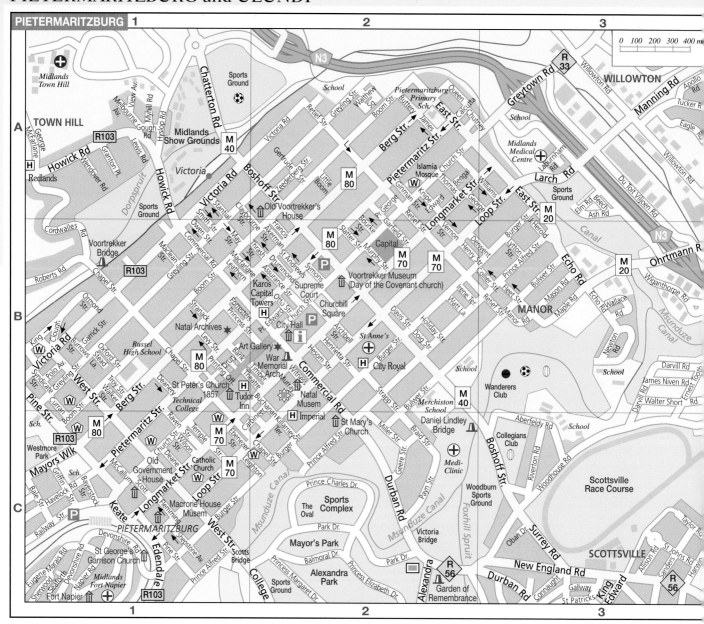

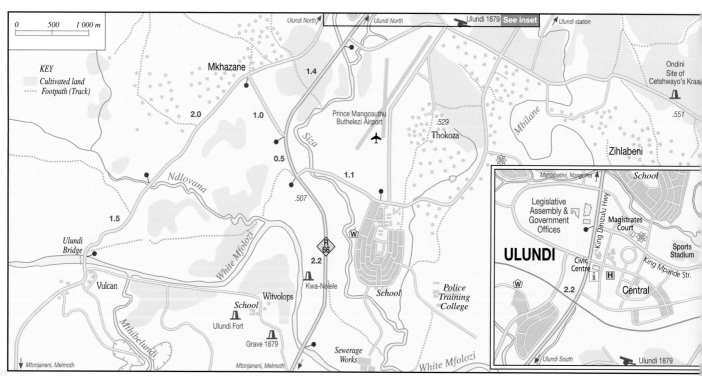

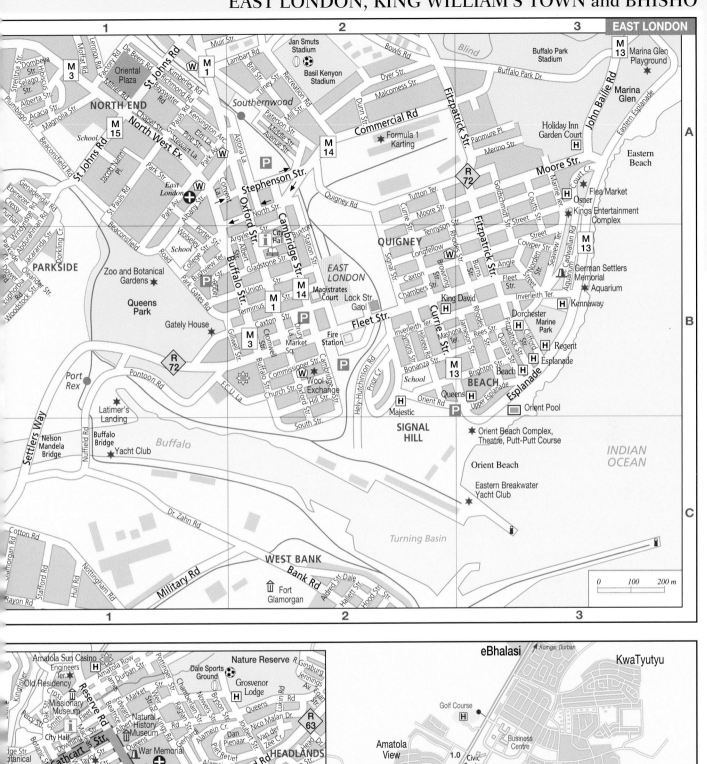

EAST LONDON

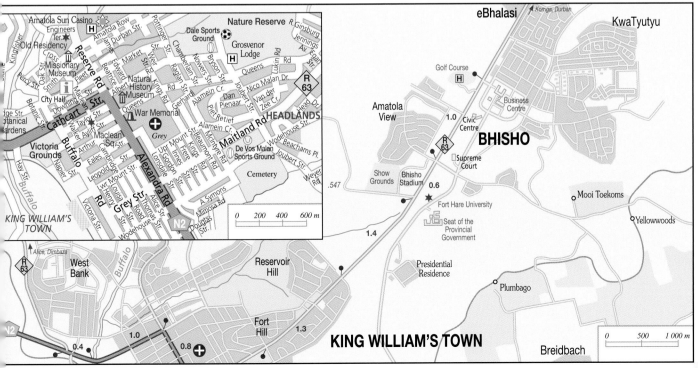

KING WILLIAM'S TOWN

BHISHO

PORT ELIZABETH and ENVIRONS

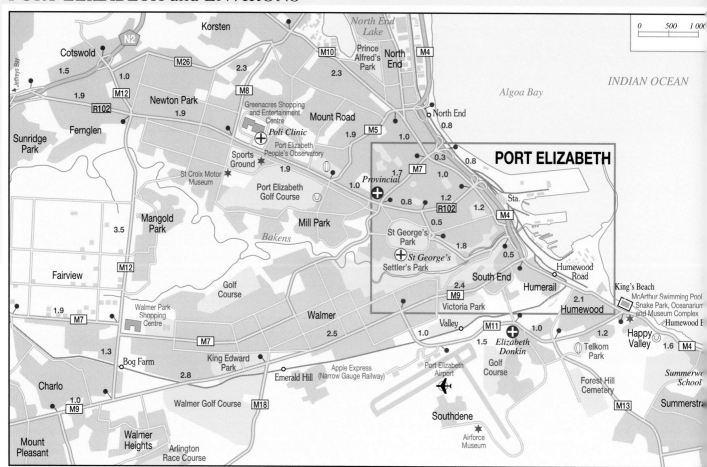

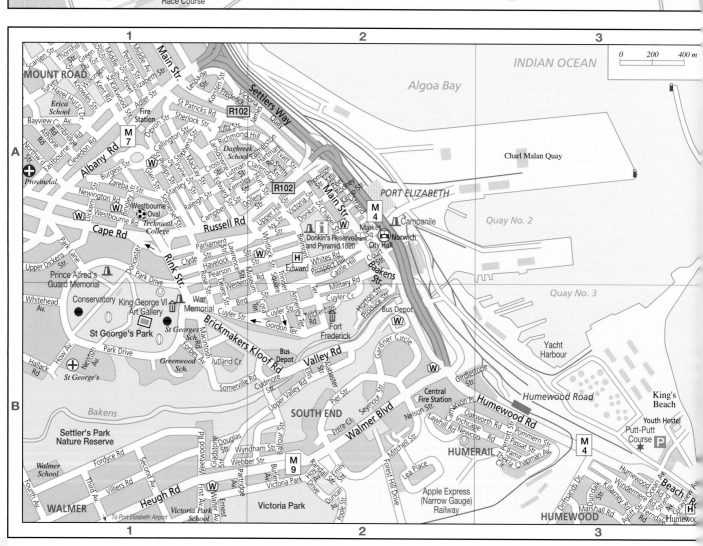

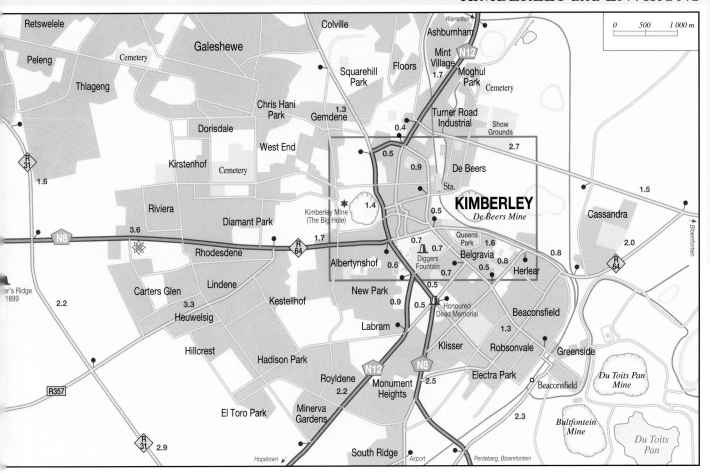

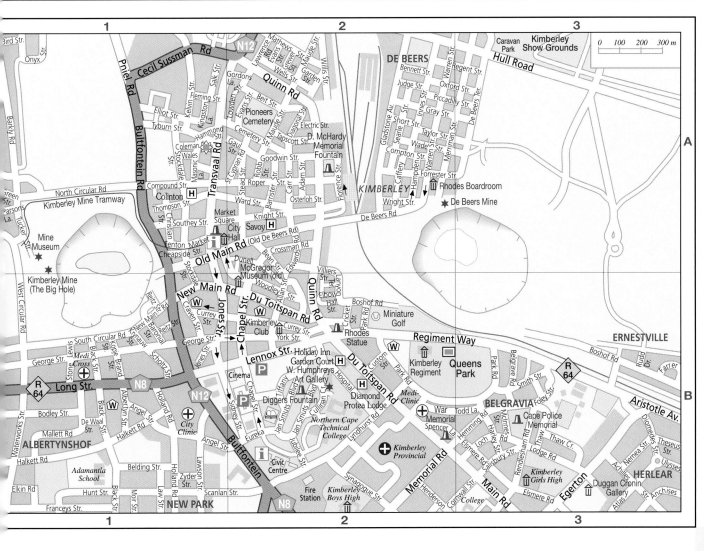

MAFIKENG and ENVIRONS

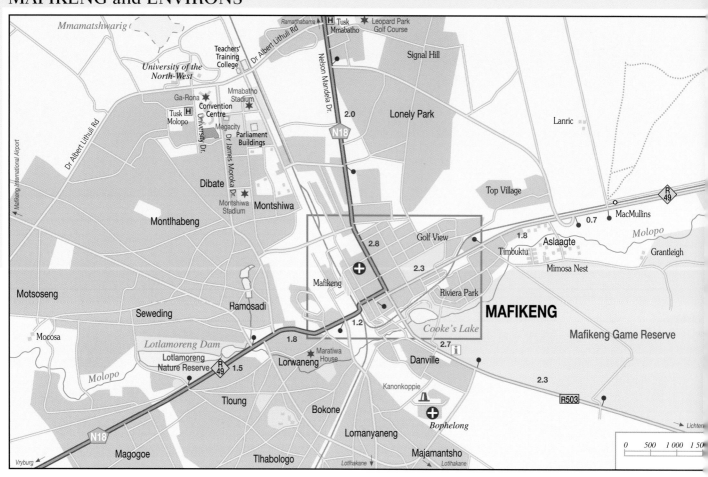

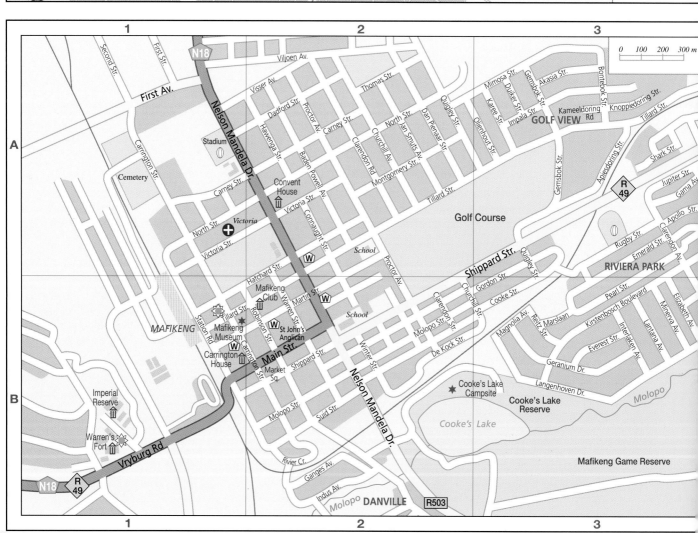

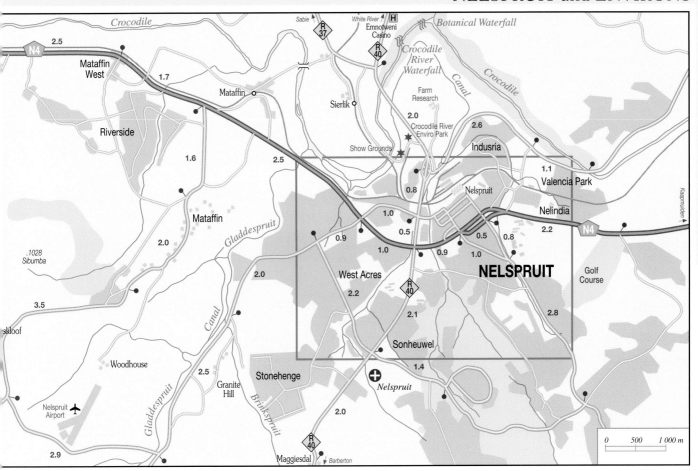

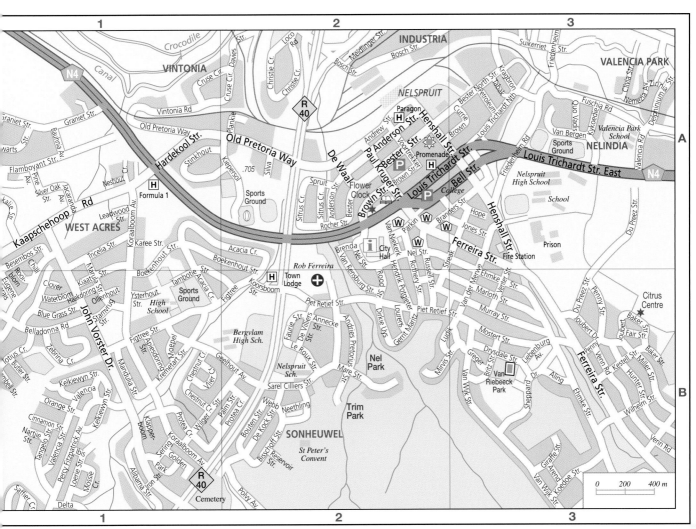

POLOKWANE (PIETERSBURG) and ENVIRONS

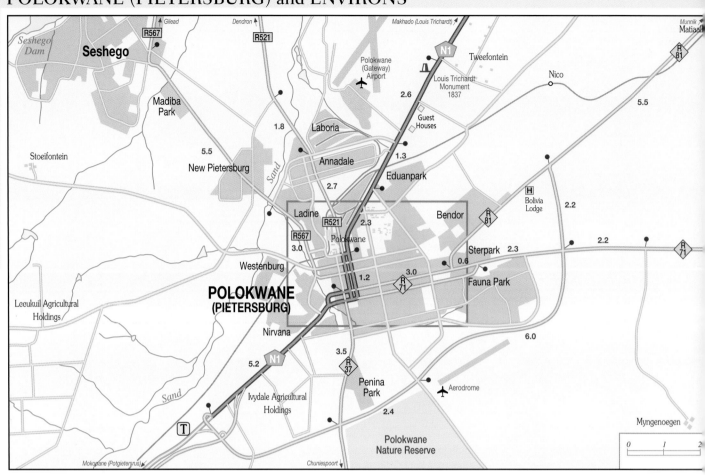

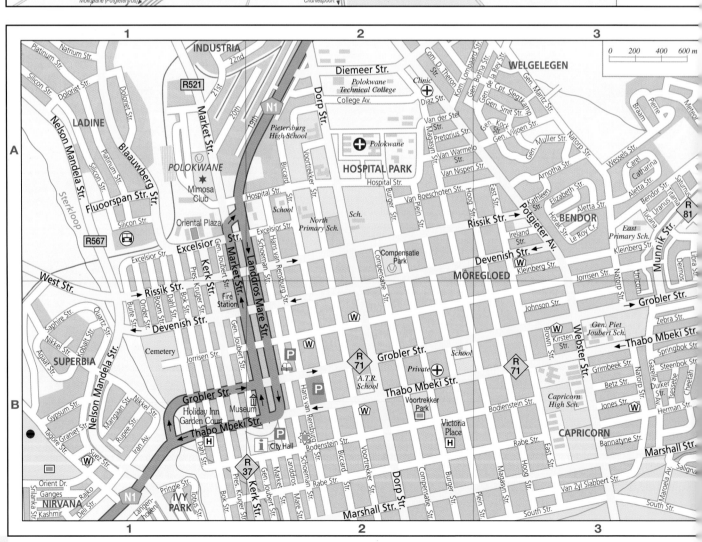

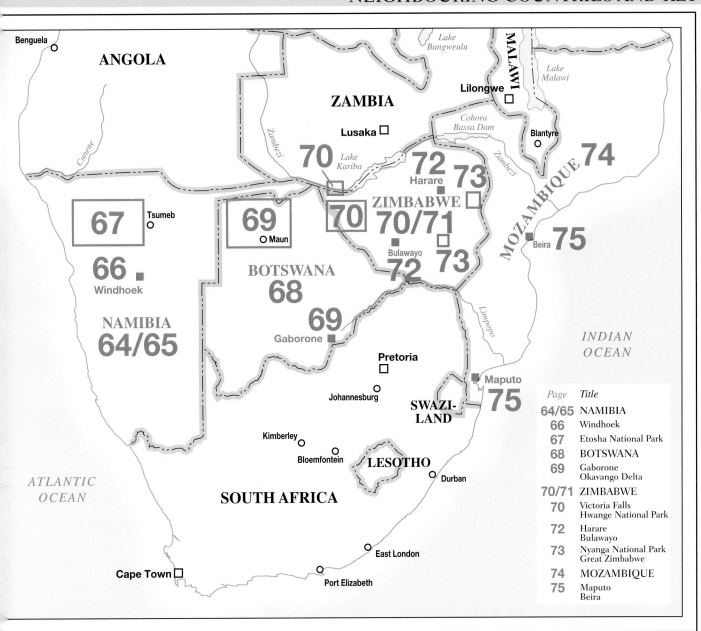

Page	Title
64/65	NAMIBIA
66	Windhoek
67	Etosha National Park
68	BOTSWANA
69	Gaborone Okavango Delta
70/71	ZIMBABWE
70	Victoria Falls Hwange National Park
72	Harare Bulawayo
73	Nyanga National Park Great Zimbabwe
74	MOZAMBIQUE
75	Maputo Beira

KEY

Motorway		Railway		National airport	✈
National road		International boundary		Airport and airfield	✈ ✚
Main road	surfaced gravel	Nature reserve		Chalet/holiday resort	
Secondary road	surfaced gravel	City with built-up area		Hotel	H
Route numbers	B1 C28 D620	City	□	Border crossing	✕ Vioolsdrif
4x4 track		Major town	○	Place of interest	✳ Picnic area
Distance in kilometres	6	Secondary town	⊙	Monument	⬠
Trail		Large village	◎	Waterfall	
River, marsh and dam		Village	○	Camping ground	▲
Information centre	i	Small village or station	○	Parking	P

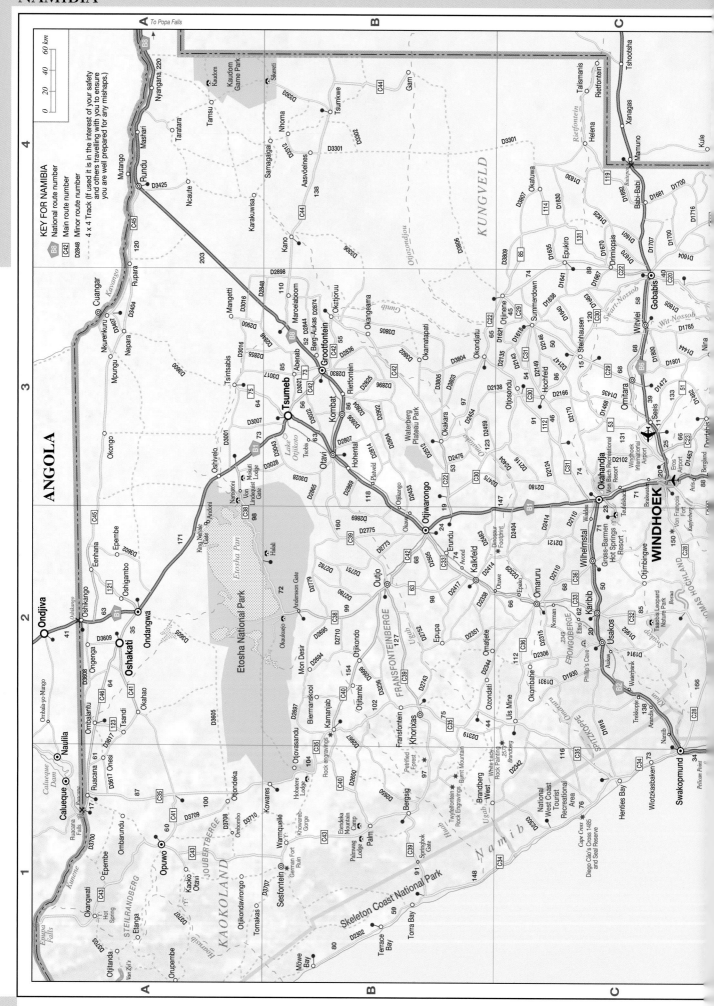

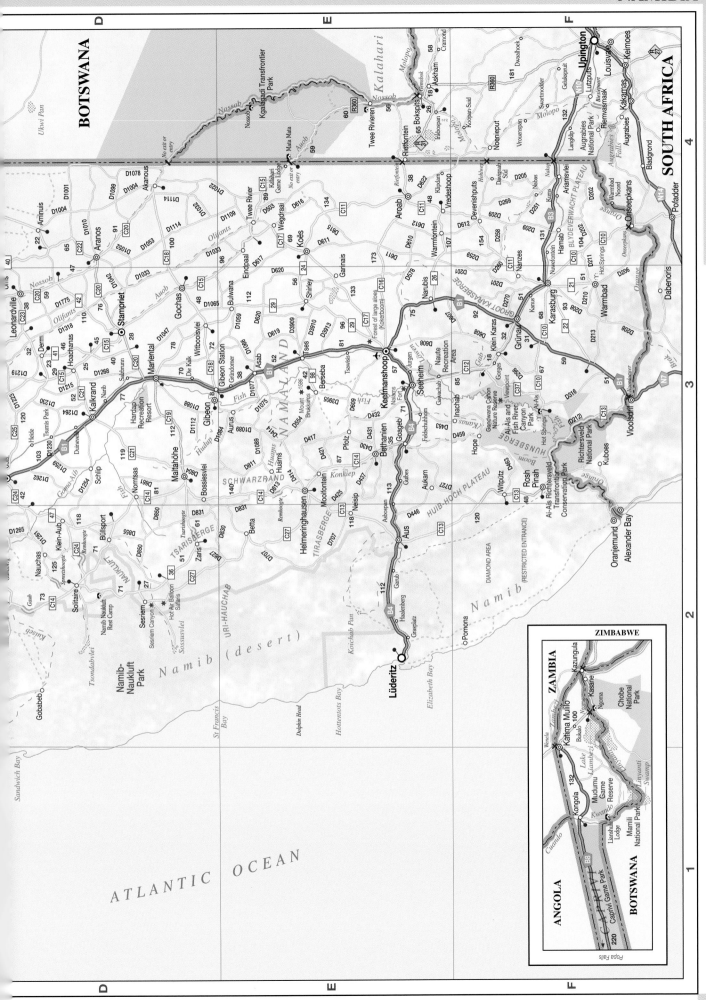

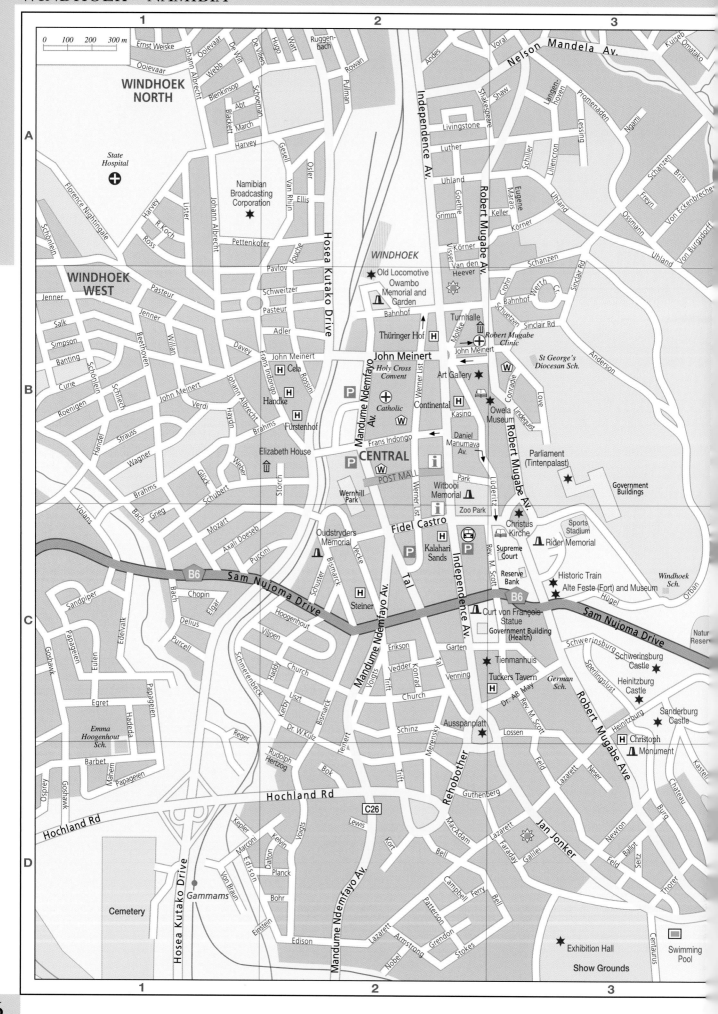

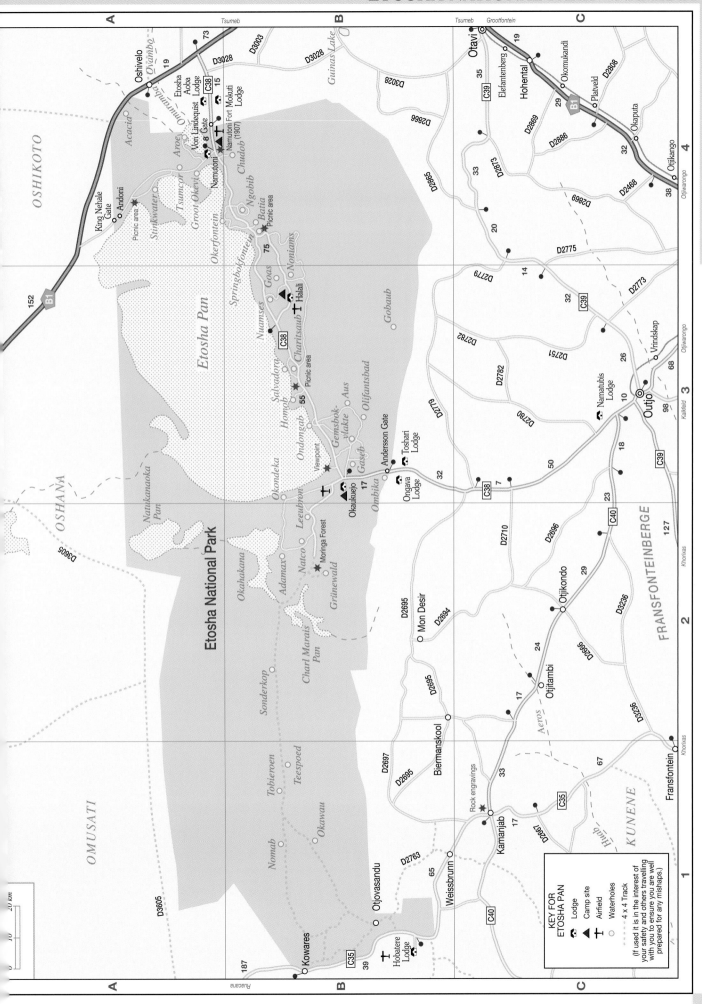

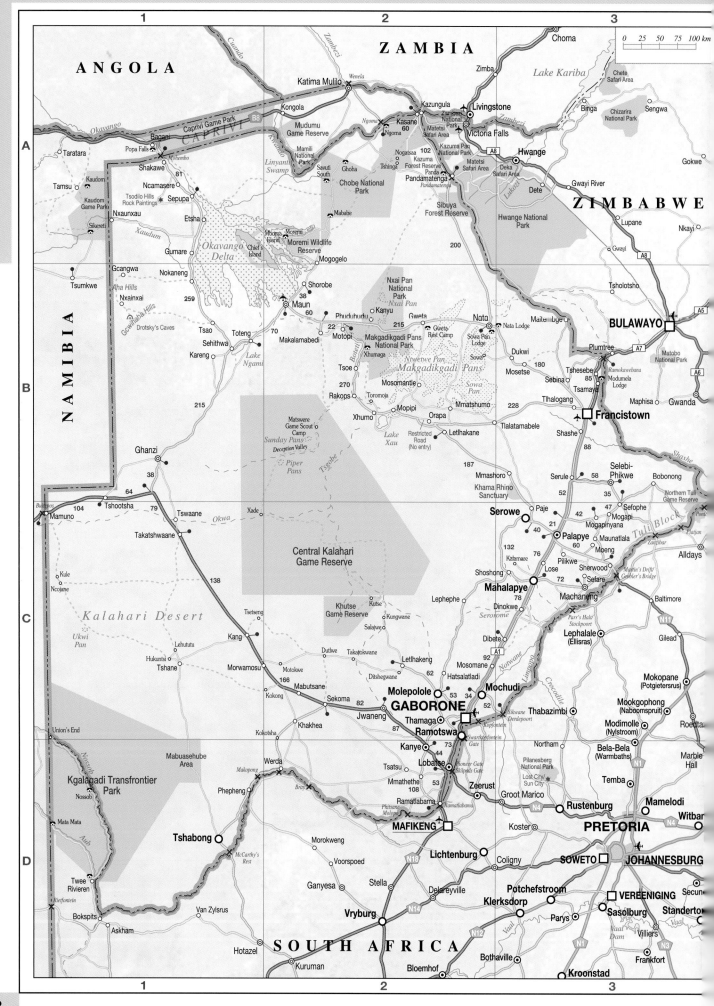

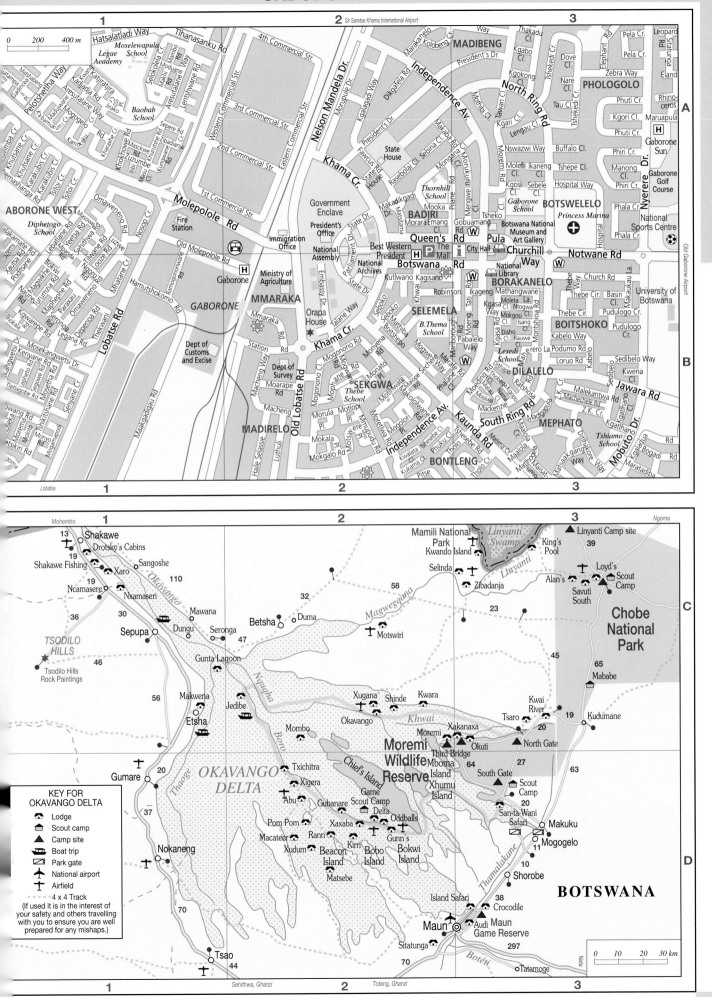

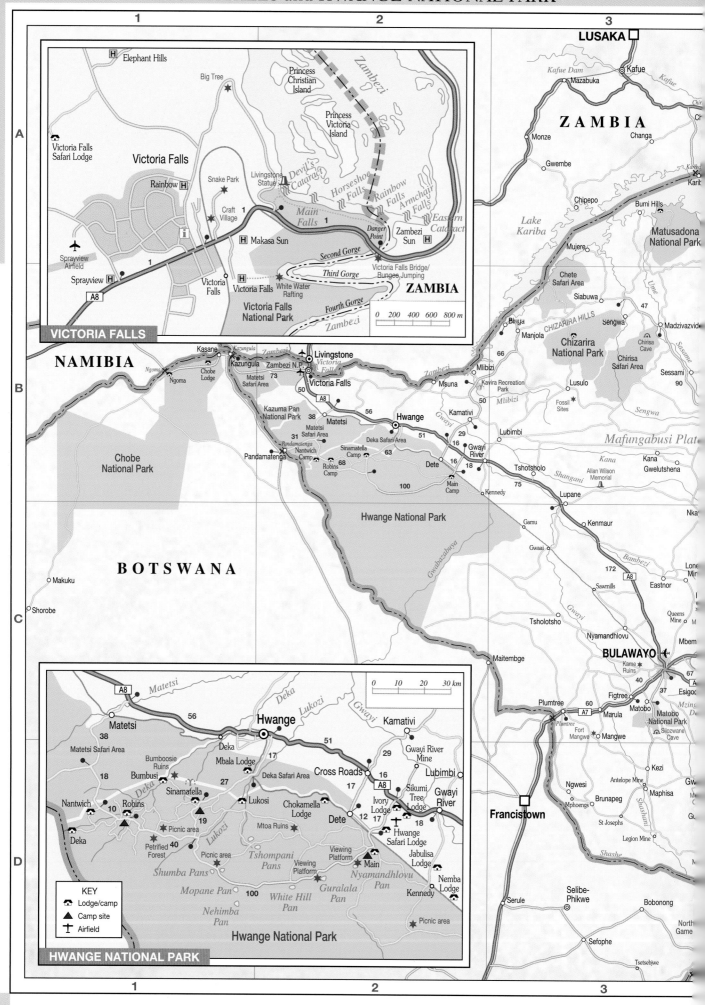

VICTORIA FALLS map inset labels:

Elephant Hills, Big Tree, Princess Christian Island, Princess Victoria Island, Zambezi, Victoria Falls Safari Lodge, Victoria Falls, Snake Park, Rainbow, Craft Village, Livingstone Statue, Devil's Cataract, Horseshoe Falls, Rainbow Falls, Armchair Falls, Eastern Cataract, Main Falls, Danger Point, Makasa Sun, Zambezi Sun, Sprayview Airfield, Second Gorge, Third Gorge, Victoria Falls Bridge/Bungee Jumping, ZAMBIA, Sprayview, Victoria Falls, Victoria Falls, White Water Rafting, Fourth Gorge, Victoria Falls National Park, Zambezi, A8

0 200 400 600 800 m

VICTORIA FALLS

Main map labels:

LUSAKA, Kafue Dam, Kafue, Mazabuka, Kafue, ZAMBIA, Monze, Changa, Gwembe, Chipepo, Burni Hills, Karit, Lake Kariba, Matusadona National Park, Mujere, Madzivazvido, Chete Safari Area, 47, Siabuwa, Chirisa Cave, Chizarira Hills, Sengwa, Chirisa Safari Area, Binga, Manjola, Chizarira National Park, Sessami, 90, Mlibizi, 66, Kavira Recreation Park, Lusulo, Msuna, 50, Mlibizi, Fossil Sites, Sengwa, Kasane, Kazungula, Zambezi, Livingstone, Victoria Falls, Zambezi, Mafungabusi Plat, NAMIBIA, Kazungula, Zambezi N.P., Victoria Falls, Ngoma, Chobe Lodge, Matetsi Safari Area, 73, 50, A8, 56, Hwange, Kamativi, Kana, Kana, Gwelutshena, Ngoma, Kazuma Pan National Park, 38, Matetsi, 51, 29, Lubimbi, Allan Wilson Memorial, Shangani, Pandamatenga, Matetsi Safari Area, 31, Nantwich Camp, Sinamatella Camp, Deka Safari Area, 63, 16, Gwayi River, Tshotsholo, Chobe National Park, Robins Camp, 68, Dete, 16, 18, 75, Lupane, 100, Main Camp, Kennedy, Gamu, Kenmaur, Nka, Hwange National Park, Gwaai, BOTSWANA, Gwabarabuya, Gwaai, Bamberzi, 172, A8, Lone Min, Makuku, Sawmills, Eastnor, Shorobe, Tsholotsho, Queens Mine, Nyamandhlovu, Mbem, Maitembge, BULAWAYO, Kame Ruins, 40, 67, Figtree, 37, Esigod, Plumtree, 60, A7, Marula, Matobo, Matobo National Park, Plumtree, Fort Mangwe, Mangwe, Silozwane Cave, Kezi, Ngwesi, Antelope Mine, Maphisa, Gw, Mphoengs, Brunapeg, Gu, St Josephs, Legion Mine, Gu

HWANGE NATIONAL PARK inset labels:

A8, Matetsi, Deka, Lukozi, Gwayi, 56, Matetsi, Hwange, Kamativi, Matetsi Safari Area, Deka, 17, 51, 29, Gwayi River Mine, Bumboosie Ruins, Mbala Lodge, Deka Safari Area, Cross Roads, 16, Lubimbi, Bumbusi, 18, 27, 17, A8, Sinamatella, Lukosi, Chokamella Lodge, Sikumi Tree Lodge, Gwayi River, Nantwich, 10, Robins, 19, Mtoa Ruins, Ivory Lodge, 12, 17, Deka, Picnic area, Petrified Forest, 40, Picnic area, Tshompani Pans, Viewing Platform, Dete, Hwange Safari Lodge, Jabulisa Lodge, Francistown, Shumba Pans, Lukozi, Mopane Pan, Viewing Platform, Nyamandhlovu Pan, Guralala Pan, Kennedy, Nemba Lodge, Serule, Selibe-Phikwe, Bobonong, Nehimba Pan, 100, White Hill Pan, Hwange National Park, Sefophe, North Game, Tsetsejbwe

0 10 20 30 km

KEY
- 🏠 Lodge/camp
- ▲ Camp site
- ✝ Airfield

HWANGE NATIONAL PARK

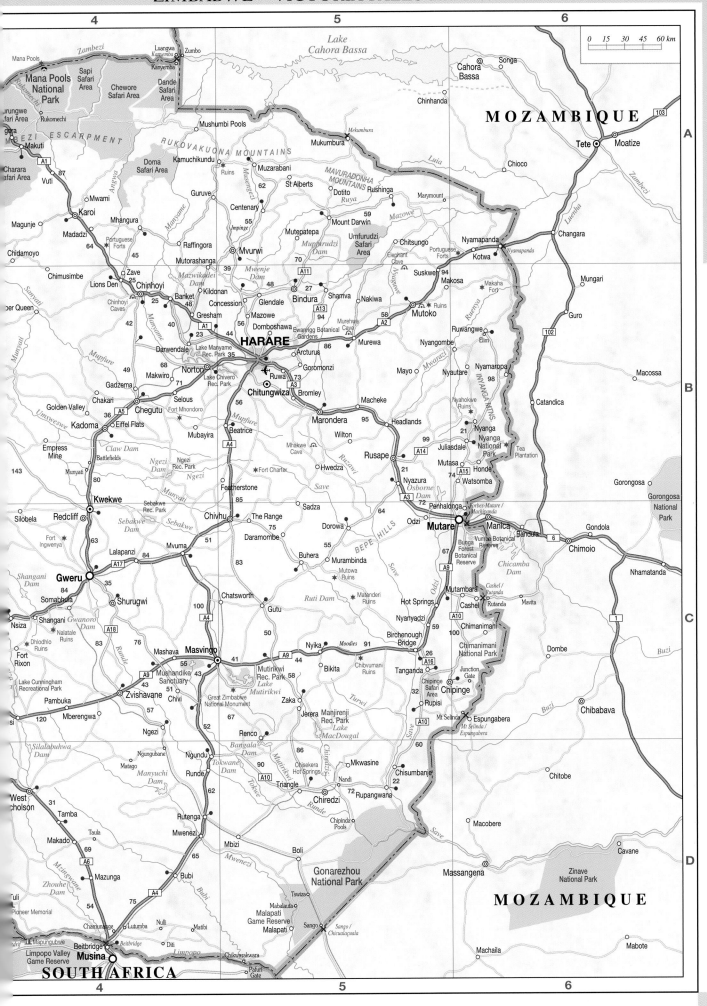

HARARE and BULAWAYO – ZIMBABWE

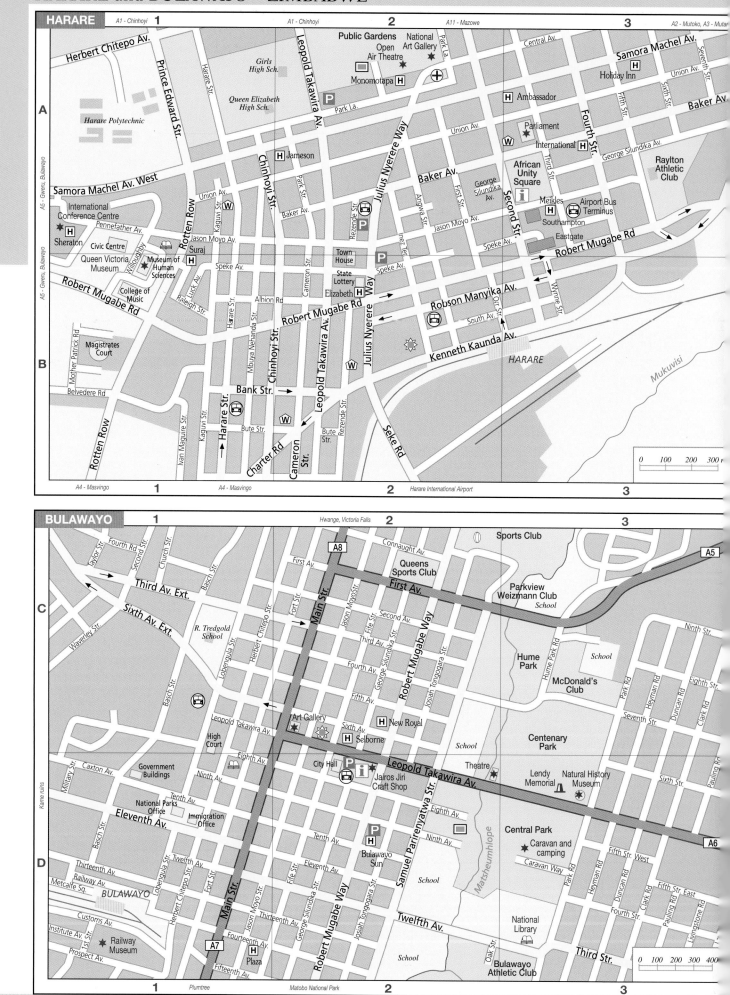

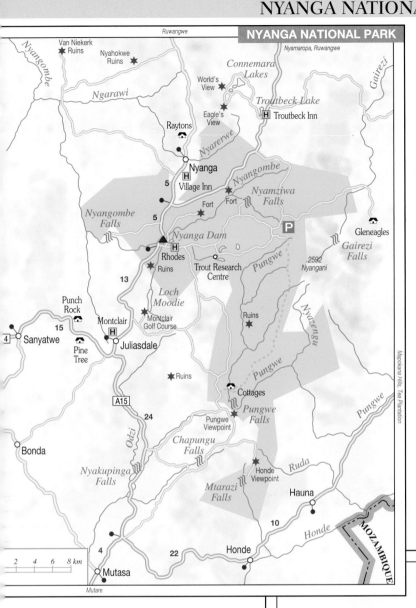

Ruwangwe

Van Niekerk Ruins
Nyahokwe Ruins
Ngarawi
Nyangombe

Nyamaropa, Ruwangwe
Connemara Lakes
Gairezi
World's View
Troutbeck Lake
Eagle's View
Troutbeck Inn H
Raytons
Nyarerwe
Nyanga H
Village Inn
5
Fort
Fort
Nyangombe
Nyamziwa Falls
Nyangombe Falls
5
Nyanga Dam H
Rhodes
Ruins
Trout Research Centre
Pungwe
.2592 Nyangani
Gleneagles
Gairezi Falls
13
Loch Moodie
Ruins
Nyazengu
Punch Rock
15
Montclair H
Montclair Golf Course
4
Sanyatwe
Juliasdale
Pine Tree
Ruins
Pungwe
A15
Ruins
Cottages
24
Pungwe Falls
Pungwe
Pungwe Viewpoint
Chapungu Falls
Odzi
Honde Viewpoint
Ruda
Pungwe
Bonda
Nyakupinga Falls
Mtarazi Falls
Hauna
10
Honde
2 4 6 8 km
4
22
Honde
MOZAMBIQUE
Mutasa
Mutare

Mapokana Hills, Tea Plantation

Mtarazi Falls in the Nyanga National Park, Eastern Highlands

Zimbabwe National Monument near Masvingo

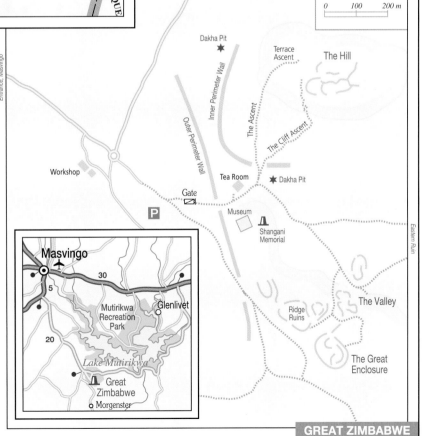

Masvinga to Lake Mutirikwa Road

0   100   200 m

Dakha Pit
Terrace Ascent
The Hill
The Ascent
Inner Perimeter Wall
The Cliff Ascent
Outer Perimeter Wall
Entrance, Masvingo
Workshop
Tea Room
Dakha Pit
Gate
Museum
P
Shangani Memorial
Eastern Ruin

Masvingo
30
5
Glenlivet
Mutirikwa Recreation Park
20
Ridge Ruins
The Valley
Lake Mutirikwa
Great Zimbabwe
Morgenster
The Great Enclosure

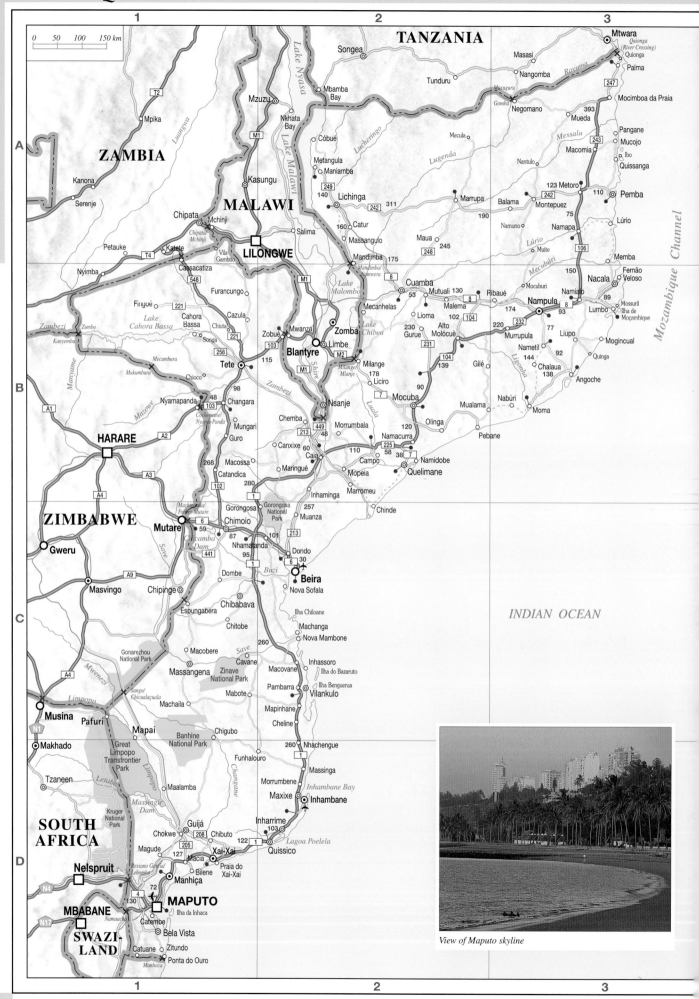

View of Maputo skyline

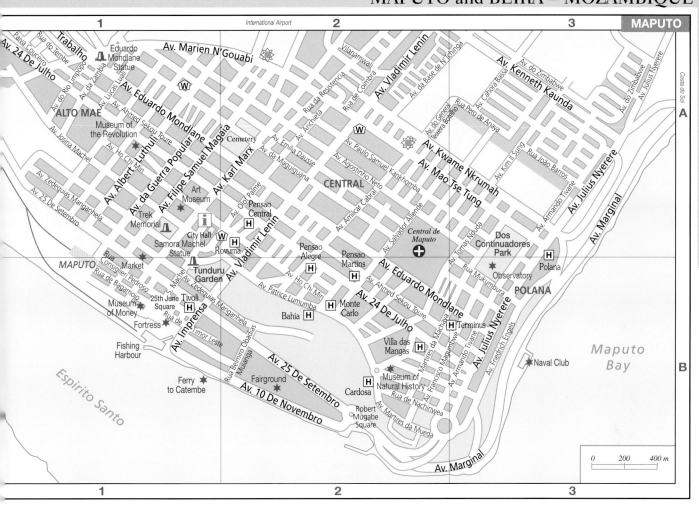

MAPUTO

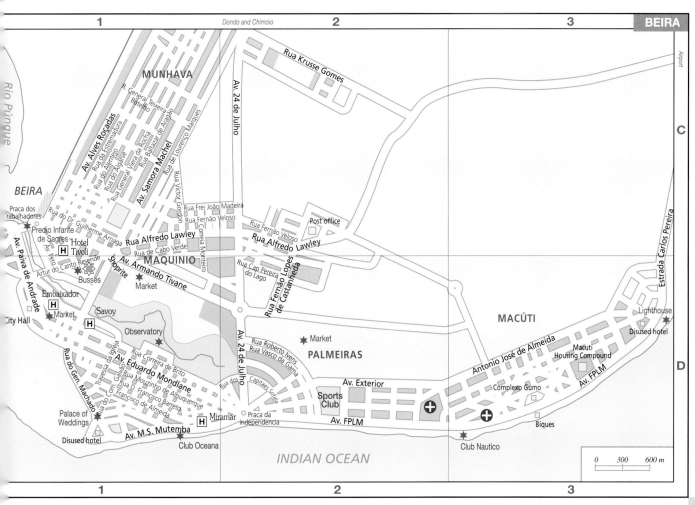

BEIRA

PLACE NAMES INDEX

A

	Page
Abbotsdale	4 C 1
Abbotspoort	20 B 2
Abercorn Drift	19 C 6
Aberdeen Road	6 B 1
Aberdeen	6 B 1
Aberfeldy	18 D 2
Acacia	5 A 5
Acornhoek	21 C 5
Addo	6 C 2
Adelaide	6 B 3
Adendorp	6 A 1
Afguns	20 C 2
Afrikaskop	18 D 2
Aggeneys	9 B 4
Agtergang	11 C 5
Ahrens	13 A 4
Ai-Ais	14 D 3
Airlie	19 A 4
Albert Falls	13 B 4
Albertinia	5 D 4
Alberton	18 B 2
Alcockspruit	18 D 3
Aldam	12 A 1
Alexander Bay	8 A 1
Alexandria	6 C 3
Algeria	4 A 2
Algiers	16 B 3
Alheit	9 A 5
Alice	7 B 4
Alicedale	6 C 3
Aliwal North	11 C 6
Allandale	12 A 1
Allanridge	17 D 6
Alldays	20 A 3
Alma	20 C 2
Aloeridge	5 C 4
Amalia	17 C 4
Amandelboom	9 D 6
Amanzimtoti	13 C 5
aMatikulu	13 A 5
Amerika	18 D 1
Amersfoort	18 C 3
Ammerville	5 A 4
Amsterdam	19 B 4
Andrieskraal	6 C 1
Andriesvale	15 C 6
Ann's Villa	6 B 3
Anysspruit	19 C 4
Arboretum	13 A 6
Argent	18 B 2
Ariamsvlei	15 D 5
Ariesfontein	10 A 3
Arlington	18 D 1
Aroab	15 C 5
Arundel	11 D 4
Asab	14 A 3
Asbospan	14 C 2
Ascent	18 C 2
Ashburton	13 B 4
Ashton	4 C 3
Askeaton	12 D 1
Askham	15 C 6
Assegaaibos	6 C 1
Assen	18 A 1
Aston Bay	6 C 2
Atamelang	17 C 5
Atlanta Sta.	20 D 2
Atlanta	18 A 1
Atlantis	4 C 1
Atteridgeville	18 A 1
Attie	18 C 1
Augrabies	9 A 5
Aukam	14 C 2
Aurora	4 B 1
Aurus	14 A 3
Aus	14 C 1
Ausnek	14 C 2
Aussenkehr	8 A 2
Austin's Post	11 B 5
Ausweiche	14 C 1
Avondrus	4 C 3
Avondster	17 C 5
Avontuur	5 C 6

B

	Page
Baardskeerdersbos	4 D 2
Babanango	13 A 5
Badplaas	19 B 4
Baikhutso	17 B 5
Bailey	6 A 3
Baines Drift	20 A 3
Bakenberg	20 C 3
Bakenklip	10 D 1
Bakerville	17 B 5
Balfour	18 C 2
Balfour	6 B 3
Balgowan	13 B 4
Balkfontein	17 C 6
Ballengeich	18 D 3
Ballito	13 B 5
Balmoral	18 B 2
Baltimore	20 B 3
Bandelierkop	21 B 4
Bandur	21 A 4
Bankies	11 D 6
Banksvlei	9 A 5
Banner's Rest	13 D 4
Bapong	18 A 1
Bapong	20 D 1
Bapsfontein	18 B 2
Barandas	5 C 6
Barberspan	17 B 5
Barberton	19 B 4
Barkly East	12 D 1
Barkly Pass	12 D 2
Barkly West	11 A 4
Baroda	6 A 2
Baroe	6 B 1
Barrington	5 C 6
Barrydale	4 C 3
Bashibisi	13 A 6
Bathurst	7 C 4
Batlharo	16 C 3
Baviaanskrans	17 C 6
Bayala	19 D 6
Baynesfield	13 B 4
Beacon Bay	7 B 5
Beaufort West	5 A 5
Beauty	20 B 2
Beauvallon	8 A 1
Bedford	6 B 3
Beesbank	8 A 2
Beeshoek	10 A 2
Beeshoek	16 D 2
Beestekraal	18 A 1
Beeswater	8 D 3
Beitbridge	21 A 4
Bela Vista	19 B 6
Bela-Bela (Les.)	12 A 2
Bela-Bela	20 D 3
Belfast	18 A 3
Belfast	21 D 6
Belgrave	12 C 2
Bell	21 C 4
Bellsbank Mine	17 D 4
Bellville	4 C 1
Belmont	11 B 4
Bendell	16 C 3
Benoni	18 B 2
Bensonvale	12 C 1
Berbice	19 C 5
Berg River	4 B 1
Bergnek	21 C 4
Bergplaas	5 C 5
Bergsig	18 C 2
Bergsig	8 B 3
Bergville	12 A 3
Berlin	7 B 4
Bermolli	10 A 2
Berseba	14 B 3
Besters	12 A 3
Bethal East	18 B 3
Bethal	18 B 3
Bethanie	18 A 1
Bethanie, Namibia	14 B 2
Bethelsdorp	6 C 2
Bethesda Road	6 A 2
Bethlehem	12 A 2
Bethulie	11 C 5
Betta	14 A 2
Betty's Bay	4 D 2
Bewaarkloof	21 C 4
Bhadeni	19 C 4
Bhalekane	19 B 5
Bhaziya	7 A 5
Bhekuzulu	19 D 4
Bhisho	7 B 4
Bholo	7 A 4
Bholothwa	7 A 4
Bhunya	19 B 4
Bidiza	12 D 3
Bierspruit	20 D 1
Biesiesfontein	8 D 3
Biesiespoort	5 A 6
Biesiesvlei	17 B 5
Big Nek	19 C 5
Biggersberg	13 A 4
Bisi	13 C 4
Bitterfontein	8 D 3
Bityi	7 A 5
Bizana	13 D 4
Black Rock	16 C 2
Blackheath	17 B 4

	Page
Bladgrond	9 A 5
Blanco	5 C 5
Blandsdrift	5 D 4
Bleakmoor	7 B 4
Bleskop	18 A 1
Blesmanspos	17 D 4
Bletterman	11 C 4
Blikfontein	16 D 3
Blikpan	18 B 3
Blinkpan	18 B 2
Blinkwater	21 B 4
Bloekomspruit	18 C 2
Bloemfontein	11 A 6
Bloemhof	17 D 5
Blood River	19 D 4
Blouberg	20 B 3
Bloubergstrand	4 C 1
Bloudrif	17 D 6
Bluegums	12 C 1
Bluewater Bay	6 C 2
Blydskap	18 D 2
Blythedale Beach	13 B 5
Blyvooruitsig	9 B 4
Boane	19 B 6
Bodenstein	17 B 6
Bodiam	7 C 4
Bodibe	17 B 5
Boegoeberg	10 A 2
Boerboonfontein	4 C 3
Boesmanskop	11 C 6
Boetsap	17 D 4
Bogogobo	16 C 1
Bogwasa	21 C 5
Bohlokong	18 D 2
Boipelo	17 D 4
Boitshoko	10 A 3
Boitumelong	17 D 5
Bokaa	20 A 1
Bokkoppie	16 D 2
Bokkraal	17 B 6
Boknes	6 C 3
Boksburg	18 B 2
Bokspits	15 C 6
Bolahlakgomo	21 C 4
Bollantlokwe	18 A 1
Bolokaneng	11 B 5
Bon Accord	18 A 2
Bongolethu	5 C 5
Bonnievale	4 C 3
Bonteheuwel	10 D 2
Bontebok	20 B 1
Bonwapitse	20 B 1
Boomplaas	12 D 1
Boons	18 B 1
Boord	18 A 3
Borakalalo	17 A 5
Borolelo	17 A 6
Bosbult	21 B 4
Boshoek	17 A 6
Boshof	11 A 5
Boskop	17 B 6
Boskuil	17 C 5
Bospoort	17 B 5
Bossies	17 B 5
Bossiesvlei	14 A 2
Bosterlea	11 D 6
Boston	13 B 4
Bot River	4 D 2
Bothaspas	18 D 3
Bothaville	17 C 6
Bothithong	16 C 3
Botleng	18 B 2
Botshabelo	11 B 6
Bourke's Luck	21 C 5
Bo-Wadrif	4 B 3
Boyateng	18 A 1
Braemar	13 C 4
Brakbos	10 B 1
Brakpan	18 B 2
Brakpoort	10 D 3
Brakspruit	17 C 6
Brandfort	11 A 6
Brandkop	9 D 5
Brandrivier	5 C 4
Brandvlei	9 C 5
Brandwag	5 C 5
Braunschweig	19 C 4
Bray	16 A 3
Breakfast Vlei	7 B 4
Bredasdorp	4 D 3
Breipaal	11 C 6
Brent Park	18 D 1
Breyten	18 B 3
Bridgewater	21 B 4
Brits	20 D 2
Britstown	10 C 3
Brittania Bay	4 B 1
Britten	17 D 5
Broedersput	17 C 4
Broederstroom	18 A 1

	Page
Brombeek	21 A 4
Brondal	21 D 5
Bronkhorstspruit	18 B 2
Brooks Nek	12 C 3
Brospan	9 C 6
Brukkaros	14 A 3
Bruntville	13 B 4
Bruyns Hill	13 B 4
Buckingham	17 B 6
Bucklands	10 A 3
Buffeljags Bay	4 D 2
Buffeljags River	4 C 3
Buffels Bay	5 C 6
Buffelsbank	8 B 2
Buffelsdoorn	20 C 1
Buffelsdoring	12 D 1
Buffelsdrifhek	20 B 1
Buffelsfontein	17 C 6
Buffelsfontein	6 B 2
Buffelsvlei	21 D 5
Buhlebomzinyathi	19 D 4
Buhlebomzinyathi	19 D 4
Buitenzorg	19 C 4
Bukwana	7 A 4
Bulembu	19 B 5
Bulge River	20 C 2
Bulletrap	8 B 3
Bulpan	18 A 2
Bultfontein	17 D 5
Bulwana	15 A 4
Bulwer	13 B 4
Burgersdorp	11 D 6
Burgersfort	21 C 5
Burgervilleweg	11 D 4
Burnshill	7 B 4
Bushbuckridge	21 D 5
Bushlands	19 D 6
Bushman's Nek	12 B 3
Bushmans River Mouth	6 C 3
Butha-Buthe	12 A 2
Butterworth	7 A 5
Buysdorp	21 B 4
Bylsteel	21 B 4

C

	Page
Cacadu	7 A 4
Cala Road	12 D 1
Cala	12 D 1
Caledon	4 D 2
Calitzdorp Spa	5 C 4
Calitzdorp	5 C 4
Calvert	19 D 4
Calvinia	9 D 5
Cambria	6 C 1
Cameron's Glen	6 B 3
Campbell	10 A 3
Camperdown	13 B 4
Cannon Rocks	6 C 3
Cannonvale	6 C 3
Cape Agulhas	4 D 3
Cape St Francis	6 D 2
Cape Town	4 C 1
Carletonville	18 B 1
Carlisle Bridge	6 B 3
Carlisonia	17 B 6
Carlow	21 A 4
Carlton	11 D 4
Carnarvon	10 D 2
Carolina	19 B 4
Carolusberg	8 B 3
Casteel	21 D 5
Catembe	19 B 6
Cathcart	7 A 4
Cathedral Peak	12 A 3
Cato Ridge	13 B 4
Catuane	19 C 6
Cebe	7 B 5
Cedarville	12 C 3
Cederberg	4 B 2
Cencele	12 D 1
Centane	7 B 5
Centuli	7 B 5
Centurion	18 B 2
Ceres	4 C 2
Chalumna	7 B 4
Chamchawib	14 A 2
Chamieites	14 C 3
Chamunange	21 A 4
Charl Cilliers	18 C 2
Charlestown	18 C 3
Charlesville	11 B 5
Chatsworth	13 B 5
Chicualacuala	21 A 6
Chidima	17 B 6
Chieveley	13 A 4

	Page
Chikwarakwara	21 A 5
Chintsa Mouth	7 B 5
Chintsa West	7 B 5
Choseng	17 C 4
Christiana	17 D 5
Christmas Rock	7 B 4
Chromedale	20 D 2
Churchhaven	4 B 1
Citrusdal	4 B 2
Clansthal	13 C 5
Clanville	12 D 1
Clanwilliam	4 A 2
Clarens	12 A 2
Clarkebury	7 A 5
Clarkson	6 C 1
Clewer	18 B 3
Clifford	12 D 1
Clocolan	12 A 1
Clydesdale	18 C 1
Coalville	18 B 3
Coega	6 C 2
Coenbult	14 C 3
Coerney	6 C 2
Coetzersdam	17 C 4
Coffee Bay	7 A 6
Cofimvaba	7 A 4
Coghlan	7 A 5
Colchester	6 C 3
Colcford	12 C 3
Colenso	13 A 4
Colesberg	11 C 5
Coligny	17 B 6
Committees Drift	7 B 4
Concordia	16 B 2
Concordia	8 B 3
Content	17 D 4
Conway	6 A 2
Cookhouse	6 B 3
Copperton	10 B 2
Cornelia	18 C 2
Cottage	21 C 4
Cottondale	21 C 5
Cove Rock	7 B 5
Cradock	6 A 2
Cramond	16 C 1
Crecy	11 B 5
Crocodile Bridge Gate	19 A 5
Crooks Corner	21 A 6
Cross Roads	7 B 4
Croydon	19 B 5
Cullinan	18 A 2
Cumakala	7 B 4
Curia	21 A 6
Curry's Post	13 B 4

D

	Page
Dadane	12 C 3
Dagab	9 B 5
Dagbreek	10 A 1
Daleside	18 B 1
Dalmanutha	19 A 4
Dalton	13 B 4
Dan	21 C 5
Danabaai	5 D 5
Daniëlskuil	16 D 3
Daniëlsrus	18 D 2
Daninge	7 C 4
Dannhauser	18 D 3
Dansters	12 C 1
Dargle	13 B 4
Darling	4 C 1
Darnall	13 B 5
Dassen Island	4 C 1
Dassiefontein	6 A 1
Davel	18 B 3
Daveyton	18 B 2
Davignab Süd	15 D 5
De Aar	10 C 3
De Beers	17 C 4
De Bos	4 A 2
De Brug	11 B 5
De Doorns	4 C 2
De Gracht	20 A 3
De Hoek	4 B 1
De Hoek	5 C 4
De Kelders	4 D 2
De Klerk	10 D 3
De Kol	6 C 3
De Kop	9 C 4
De Kuilen	18 C 3
De Langesdrif	18 C 3
De Rust	5 C 5
De Wildt	20 D 2

	Page
Deelpan	17 B 5
Deetlefsville	10 C 3
Delareyville	17 C 5
Delfkom	19 C 5
Delmas	18 B 2
Delportshoop	11 A 4
Deneysville	18 C 1
Dennilton	21 D 4
Deorham	16 C 3
Derby	17 B 6
Derdepoort	20 C 1
Despatch	6 C 2
Devenishputs	15 C 5
Devon	18 B 2
Devondale	17 C 4
Dewar	16 C 3
Dewetsdorp	11 B 6
Dibeng	16 D 2
Dibeng	20 B 3
Dibete	20 B 1
Die Dam	4 D 2
Die Hoek	5 C 6
Die Vlug	5 C 6
Diemansput	9 B 6
Diepdrif	9 D 5
Diepkloof	5 C 5
Diepwalle	5 C 6
Dikabeya	20 A 2
Dikgale	21 D 4
Dimbaza	7 B 4
Dindela	18 A 3
Dingapong	21 C 5
Dinkwaneng	17 D 4
Dinokana	17 A 5
Dinokwe	20 B 1
Dinopeng	16 C 3
Dinuzulu	13 A 5
Dipelaneng	12 B 1
Diphuti	21 C 5
Dirkiesdorp	19 C 4
Dirkiesrus	17 B 4
Disaneng	17 B 4
Dithakong	16 C 3
Dithakong	17 B 5
Diti	21 A 5
Ditlhake	11 B 4
Ditloung	16 D 2
Ditshipeng	16 C 3
Dkoyi	12 D 1
Dlowana	13 A 5
Dominionville	17 C 6
Dondotsha	13 A 6
Donkerpoort	11 C 5
Donnybrook	13 B 4
Doornfontein	20 D 2
Doornkraal	13 A 4
Dordrecht	12 D 1
Doring Bay	4 A 1
Doringbos	4 A 2
Doringbult	17 B 5
Doringkop	13 B 5
Dorset	20 C 3
Douglas	10 A 3
Douglas	18 B 3
Dover	18 C 1
Downes	9 D 5
Draaiberg	6 B 1
Draaikraal	18 A 3
Draghoender	10 B 2
Drakensberg Garden	12 A 3
Drakensberg Sun	12 A 3
Draycott	12 A 3
Drayton	4 D 2
Driebad	11 C 5
Driefontein	12 A 3
Driefontein	16 B 3
Driefontein	19 C 4
Driehoek	17 B 5
Driekop Mine	21 C 4
Driekoppies	19 A 5
Driver's Drift	7 A 4
Droëputs	10 D 1
Droërivier	5 A 5
Droëspruit	16 D 2
Droëvlakte	5 D 4
Droëvlei	5 C 4
Drummondlea	20 C 3
Dry Harts	17 C 4
Dudfield	17 B 5
Dududu	13 C 4
Duikersdal	10 A 2
Duiwelskloof	21 B 4
Dukathole	11 C 6
Dullstroom	21 D 4
Dumbe	19 C 4
Dumisa	13 C 4
Dundee	19 D 4

	Page
Dundonald	19 B 4
Dupleston	11 C 6
Dupperspos	17 B 6
Durban North	13 B 5
Durban	13 B 5
Durbanville	4 C 1
Dutywa	7 A 5
Dwaal	11 D 4
Dwaalboom	20 D 1
Dwaalhoek	16 D 1
Dwaleni	19 C 5
Dwarsberg	17 A 6
Dwarskersbos	4 B 1
Dwesa	18 B 2
Dwesa	7 A 6
Dweshula	13 C 4
Dwyka	5 B 4
Dysselsdorp	5 C 5
Dzanani	21 A 4

E

	Page
E'Thembeni	10 B 2
East London	7 B 5
Eastpoort	6 B 3
Eastwolds	13 C 4
Ebenhaeser	8 D 3
eBhuga	19 A 5
Edashi	12 B 3
Edenburg	11 B 5
Edendale	13 B 4
Edengrove	13 B 4
Edenvale	18 B 2
Edenville	18 D 1
Eendekuil	4 B 2
Eensgevonden	11 A 6
Eeram	18 D 2
Eerste River	4 C 1
Egham	16 B 3
Eidsamub	14 A 3
Eindpaal	15 A 4
Ekangala	18 A 2
Ekhandizwe	19 A 5
Eksteenfontein	8 A 2
eKulindeni	19 B 4
Ekuphumleni	7 A 4
eKuvukeni	13 A 4
Elands Bay	4 A 1
Elands Heights	12 D 2
Elandsdrift	11 A 4
Elandshoek	19 A 4
Elandskop	13 B 4
Elandslaagte	13 A 4
Elandsputte	17 B 5
Elangeni	13 B 4
Eldorado	20 A 3
Eleasar	17 C 6
Elgin	4 D 2
Elim	21 B 4
Elim	4 D 2
Elliot	12 D 2
Elliotdale	7 A 5
Ellisras	20 B 2
Elmeston	20 C 2
Eloff	18 B 2
eMahlubini	7 B 4
eMalahleni	18 B 3
Emantuma	19 D 6
eManzini	19 A 5
eMbalenhle	18 B 2
Embhojeni	19 A 5
Embotyi	12 D 3
Emjejane	19 A 5
Emjejane	21 D 6
eMjindini	19 B 4
eMondlo	19 D 4
Empangeni	13 A 6
eMzinoni	18 B 3
eMzinto	12 D 3
Endicott	18 B 2
eNhlalakahle	13 A 4
Ennerdale	18 B 1
Enselspruit	18 B 1
Enselsrus	17 B 5
Enterprise	20 B 2
eNtshatshongo	7 A 5
eNtsimekweni	12 C 1
Entumeni	13 A 5
Enzelsberg	18 B 1
Erasmia	18 B 1
Ermelo	18 B 3
Erts	18 B 3
Erts	21 D 4
Eshowe	13 A 5
Esibayeni	19 A 5
Esigodini	19 A 4
eSikhawini	13 A 6
eSilobela	19 B 4
eSizameleni	19 C 4

Eskdale 16 C 3
Espagsdrif 17 D 4
Estancia 18 B 3
Estcourt 13 A 4
Eston 13 A 4
Ethandakukhanya 19 C 4
Etikhulungwane 19 B 4
Etwatwa 18 B 2
Eureka 16 C 3
Evander 18 B 2
Evaton 18 B 1
Excelsior 12 A 1
eXwili 7 A 5
Ezakheni 13 A 4
eZamokuhle 18 C 3
eZibeleni 7 A 4
eZitandini 7 A 5
Ezulwini 19 B 5

F

Fafung 18 A 1
Falkenhorst 14 A 3
Fallodon 7 C 4
Fanie's Island 19 D 6
Fateng-Tse-Ntsho 18 D 1
Fauresmith 11 B 5
Fawn-Leas 13 B 4
Feldschuhhorn 14 C 3
Felixton 13 A 6
Ferndale 12 C 3
Fernie 19 B 4
Ferreira 11 B 6
Ficksburg 12 A 2
Firgrove 4 C 2
Fisantekraal 4 C 3
Fish Hoek 4 D 1
Fish River 6 A 2
Flagstaff 12 D 3
Florisbad 11 A 5
Floukraal 12 D 1
Fochville 18 B 1
Forbes Reef 19 B 5
Fort Beaufort 6 B 3
Fort Brown 6 B 3
Fort Donald 12 C 3
Fort Jackson 7 B 4
Fort Mistake 18 D 3
Fort Nottingham 13 B 4
Fountain Head 6 B 3
Fouriesburg 12 A 2
Frankfort 18 C 2
Frankfort 7 B 4
Franklin 12 D 3
Franschhoek 4 C 2
Fransenhof 10 B 2
Franskraalstrand 4 D 2
Fraser's Camp 7 C 4
Fraserburg 5 A 4
Frederickshoek 17 D 6
Frere 13 A 4
Friedenau 13 C 4
Frisgewaagd 14 B 2
Frylinckspan 16 C 2

G

Gabane 20 A 1
Gaborone 20 A 1
GaDikgale 20 B 3
Gainachas 14 A 3
GaKomape 21 B 4
Galeshewe 11 A 4
Galeshewe 11 A 4
Ga-Luka 20 D 2
GaMabelebele 20 A 3
GaMabitsha 20 B 3
GaMabotsa 21 C 4
GaMaja 21 C 4
Ga-Malwane 21 C 5
Ga-Mamatlhola 21 C 5
GaMametsa 21 C 5
GaMankgodi 20 B 3
GaMankopane 21 C 4
GaMantlhodi 20 B 3
GaMasemola 21 C 4
GaMathiba 21 C 4
GaMathule 21 C 4
GaMatlala 21 B 4
Ga-Matshogo 17 A 5
GaMatswe 21 C 5
GaModipana 20 C 3
Gamoep 8 B 3
Ga-Mogopa 17 B 6
GaMolekwa 20 B 3
GaMolepo 21 C 4
GaMonyebodi 20 B 3

Ga-Mopedi 16 C 3
Gamoswaana 17 A 5
GaMotlana 20 C 3
Ga-Motlatla 17 B 6
Ga-Motlhware 16 C 3
Ga-nala 18 B 3
Gans Bay 4 D 2
Gansfontein 4 B 2
Ganspan 17 D 4
Ganyesa 17 B 4
GaPhahla 21 C 4
Ga-Ramahlatshi 21 B 5
Ga-Ramatale 16 C 3
Ga-Ramodingwana 17 B 6
GaRamokgopa 21 B 4
Ga-Rankuwa 20 D 2
Gariep Dam 11 C 5
Garies 8 C 3
Garinals 15 B 4
Garub 14 C 1
GaSeleka 20 B 2
GaSetshaba 20 B 3
Gatberg 12 D 2
Ga-Tlhose 16 D 3
Gawachab 14 C 3
Gcina 7 A 4
Geelwal 4 A 2
Gege 19 C 4
Geluksburg 12 A 3
Geluspruit 15 D 6
Gemsbokvlakte 17 B 4
Gemsvlakte 15 D 4
Gemvale 12 D 3
Genadendal 4 C 2
Geneva 18 D 1
Gengqe 7 A 5
George 5 C 5
Gerdau 17 B 5
Germiston 18 B 2
Geysdorp 17 B 5
Gibeon Station 14 A 3
Gibeon 14 A 3
Gilead 20 B 3
Gingindlovu 13 A 5
Giyani 21 B 5
Glaudina 17 C 5
Glen Cowie 21 D 4
Glen Echo 13 C 4
Glen Harmony 17 D 6
Glen Mill 13 B 5
Glen Muir 7 B 5
Glen Thorn 6 B 3
Glen 11 A 6
Glencoe 19 D 4
Glenconnor 6 C 2
Glengarry 12 C 3
Glenmore Beach 13 D 4
Glenmore 19 B 4
Glenside 13 B 5
Glosam Park 16 D 2
Glückstadt 19 D 4
Goageb 14 C 2
Goba 19 B 6
Gobas 14 C 3
Goedemoed 11 C 6
Goedverwacht 4 B 1
Golden Fleece 17 D 6
Golden Valley 6 B 3
Goldnerville 5 B 4
Golela 19 C 5
Gonubie 7 B 5
Goodhope 17 A 5
Goodhouse 8 A 3
Goodwood 4 C 1
Gopane 17 A 5
Gordon's Bay 4 D 2
Gorges 14 D 3
Gottenburg 18 C 1
Gouda 4 C 2
Goudini 4 D 2
Gouldville 21 A 5
Gourits 5 D 4
Gouritsmond 5 D 5
Graaff-Reinet 6 A 1
Graafwater 4 A 1
Grabouw 4 D 2
Grabwasser 14 D 3
Grahamstown 6 C 3
Granaatboskolk 9 C 5
Granite 21 B 4
Graskop 21 D 5
Grasmere 18 B 1
Graspan 11 B 4
Grasplatz 14 C 1
Grass Valley Mine 21 C 4
Grauwater 15 A 4
Gravelotte 21 C 5
Great Brak River 5 C 5

Great Vaalkop Island 9 A 5
Greenlands 18 C 1
Gregory 20 A 3
Greylingstad 18 C 2
Greyton 4 C 2
Greytown 13 A 4
Griquatown 10 A 3
Groblersdal 18 A 3
Groblershoop 10 A 1
Groenberg Suid 9 C 5
Groenebloem 17 C 6
Groenkop 6 B 3
Groenpunt 18 C 1
Groenriviersmond 8 D 2
Groenvlei 19 C 4
Groot Marico 20 D 1
Groot Mier 15 C 6
Groot Waterval 5 C 4
Grootdrink 10 A 1
Grootfontein 14 A 2
Grootgeluk 20 B 2
Grootkloof 4 A 2
Grootkraal 5 C 5
Grootmis 8 B 2
Grootpan 17 B 6
Grootvlei 18 C 2
Groutville 13 B 5
Groveput 10 B 2
Gruisdrif 11 A 6
Grunau 15 D 4
Gründorner 14 A 3
Guibes 14 C 2
Gujini 13 A 4
Gumtree 12 A 1
Gunab 14 B 3
Gwiligwili 7 B 4

H

Ha Makoae 12 C 2
Haakdoring 20 C 3
Haakdoringdraai 18 A 3
Haalenberg 14 C 1
Haarlem 5 C 6
Hackney 6 A 3
HaDavhana 21 B 5
Haenertsburg 21 C 4
Haga-Haga 7 B 5
Hagesdam 11 B 5
Halane 7 A 5
Halcyon Drift 12 D 2
Halfmanshof 4 B 2
Hali 7 A 4
Hallatt's Hope 17 C 5
Hamab 15 D 5
Ha-Magoro 21 B 5
HaMakuya 21 A 5
Hamburg 7 C 4
Hammanshof 4 C 2
Hammanskraal 18 A 2
Hanaus 14 A 3
Hange 7 A 4
Hankey 6 C 2
Hanover Road 11 D 4
Hanover 11 D 4
Happy Valley 4 C 3
Ha-Rasebei 11 B 5
Hardekraaltjie 20 B 2
Harding 13 C 4
Hardup 12 D 1
Harefield 6 B 2
Harkerville 5 C 6
Harrisburg 17 C 6
Harrismith 12 A 3
Hartbeesfontein 17 C 6
Hartbeespoort 18 A 1
Hartebeeskop 19 B 4
Hartenbos 5 D 5
Hartswater 17 D 4
Haruchas 15 A 4
Hattingspruit 19 D 4
Hawerklip 18 B 2
Hawston 4 D 2
Hayfield 11 B 4
Hazel 5 A 6
Hazyview 19 A 5
Heatonville 13 A 6
Heidelberg 18 B 2
Heidelberg 5 C 4
Heilbron 18 C 1
Hekpoort 18 B 1
Helmeringhausen 14 B 2
Helpmekaar 13 A 4
Helvetia 11 B 6
Hendriksdal 19 A 4
Hendrina 18 B 3
Hennenman 17 D 6
Henning 11 D 6

Herbertsdale 5 C 4
Herefords 19 B 5
Hermanus 4 D 2
Hermanusdorings 20 C 2
Hermon 4 C 2
Herold 4 C 5
Herolds Bay 5 C 5
Herschel 12 C 1
Hertzogville 17 D 5
Het Kruis 4 B 1
Heuningneskloof 11 B 4
Heuningspruit 18 C 1
Hex River Tunnel 4 C 2
Heydon 6 A 1
Hibberdene 13 C 4
Hibernia 12 A 1
Highflats 13 C 4
Highlands 6 C 3
Himeville 12 B 3
Hlabisa 19 D 5
Hlathikhulu 19 C 5
Hlatikulu 12 B 3
Hleoheng 12 A 2
Hlobane 19 D 4
Hlobo 7 A 5
Hlogotlou 18 A 3
Hlohlo 19 A 5
Hlohlolwane 12 A 1
Hlotse (Leribe) 12 A 2
Hluhluwe 19 D 6
Hluleka 7 A 6
Hluti 19 C 5
Hobeni 7 A 6
Hobhouse 12 B 1
Hoedjies 9 D 5
Hoedspruit 21 C 5
Hoekwil 5 C 5
Hofmeyr 6 A 3
Hogsback 7 B 4
Hohane 12 D 3
Hole in the Wall 7 A 6
Holmdene 18 C 2
Holme Park 20 D 3
Holoog 14 C 3
Holy Cross 12 D 3
Hondefontein 5 A 4
Hondeklip Bay 8 C 2
Hoogte 18 C 1
Hoopstad 17 D 5
Hope 14 C 2
Hopefield 4 B 1
Hopetown 11 B 4
Hotazel 16 C 2
Houmoed 9 B 4
Hout Bay 4 C 1
Houtbosdorp 21 C 4
Houtkop 19 C 4
Houtkraal 11 C 4
Houtnek 11 A 6
Houtnek 12 A 1
Houw Hoek 4 D 2
Howick 13 B 4
Huams 14 A 2
Huhudi 17 C 4
Hukuwa 6 A 3
Humansdorp 6 C 2
Huns 14 C 2
Huntleigh 21 A 4
Hutchinson 10 D 3

I

Ibeka 7 A 5
iBhayi 6 C 2
Ifafa Beach 13 C 4
Ifafa 13 C 4
Ikageleng 17 A 5
ikageng 17 C 6
Ikhutseng 17 D 4
iLangakazi 13 A 5
Ilinge 7 A 4
Illovo Beach 13 C 5
iMbali 13 B 4
Immerpan 21 C 4
Impendle 7 A 4
Inachab 14 C 3
Inanda 13 B 5
Indemark A 20 B 3
Indwe 12 D 1
Infanta 5 D 4
iNgogo 18 D 3
Ingwavuma 19 C 5
Inhaca 19 B 6
Inkbospan 15 C 6
Inverdoorn 4 B 3
Ipelegeng 17 C 5
Ipopeng 11 B 5
Isipingo Beach 13 C 5

Isithebe 13 B 5
Iswepe 19 C 4
Ixopo 13 C 4
Izingolweni 13 D 4

J

Jacobsdal 11 B 4
Jagersfontein 11 B 5
Jamela 21 B 5
Jameson's Drift 13 A 5
Jamestown 12 D 1
Jammerdrif 12 B 1
Jan Kempdorp 17 D 4
Jane Furse 21 D 4
Jansenville 6 B 1
Jeffreys Bay 6 C 2
Jeppe's Reef 19 A 5
Jericho 18 A 1
Johannesburg 18 B 1
Johnson's Post 5 D 5
Jojweni 7 A 5
Josling 10 A 1
Joubertina 6 C 1
Jouberton 17 C 6
Jozana's Hoek 12 C 1
Jozini 19 C 6
Jujura 7 A 5
Jurgen 14 C 3

K

Kaallaagte 18 D 1
Kaapmuiden 19 A 5
Kaapsehoop 21 D 5
Kabakazi 7 B 5
Kabeana 20 C 3
KaDinga 21 B 5
Kagiso 16 B 3
KaJilongo 21 B 5
Kakamas 9 A 5
Kalbaskraal 4 C 1
Kalkbank 21 B 4
Kalkmond 9 A 5
Kalkwerf 10 A 1
KaMadonsi 21 B 5
Kamagams 14 A 2
KaMapuva 21 B 5
Kamassies 8 C 3
KaMatsakali 21 B 5
Kamatsamo 19 A 5
KaMavele 21 B 5
Kamawewe 19 B 5
KaMbokota 21 B 4
Kameel 17 B 4
KaMhinga 21 A 5
Kamieskroon 8 C 3
Kamkusi 21 A 4
Kammiebos 6 C 1
KaMphambo 21 B 5
Kamsogwaba 19 A 5
Kana 18 A 1
Kanakies 9 D 4
Kanana 17 C 6
KaNkomo 21 B 5
KaNkuzani 21 B 5
Kanoneiland 10 A 1
Kanus 15 D 4
KaNyamazane 19 A 5
Kanye 17 A 5
Karaam 15 A 4
Karasburg 15 D 4
Karatara 5 C 5
Karee 11 A 6
Kareedouw 6 C 1
Kareefontein 11 A 4
Kareekloof 10 B 3
KaRhangani 21 B 5
Karino 19 A 5
Karos 10 A 1
KaSabulane 21 B 5
Kasouga 6 C 3
Katberg 6 B 3
Katkop 9 C 5
Katlehong 18 B 2
Katse 12 B 2
Kauletsi 20 B 2
Kaya se Put 20 D 1
Ka-Xikhumba 21 B 5
Ka-Xitlakati 21 B 5
Kayser's Beach 7 B 4
Keate's Drift 13 A 4
Keetmanshoop 14 B 3
Kei Mouth 7 B 5

Kei Road 7 B 4
Keimoes 9 A 6
Keiskammahoek 7 B 4
Kelso 13 C 4
Kemp 19 C 4
Kempton Park 18 B 2
Kendal 18 B 2
Kendrew 6 B 1
Kenhardt Sta. 9 B 6
Kenhardt 10 B 1
Kenilworth 11 A 4
Kennedy's Vale 21 D 4
Kennoway 6 A 3
Kentani 7 B 5
Kenton on Sea 6 C 3
Kerkraad 5 C 5
Kestell 12 A 2
Ketane 12 C 2
Kgagodi 20 A 2
Kgalala 11 A 6
Kgobadi 17 C 4
Kgoroshi 21 B 4
Kgotsong 17 C 6
Kgubetswana 12 A 2
Khabo 12 A 2
Khadubeng 18 A 2
Khalaankomo 12 D 2
Khamisa 7 A 6
Khanyane 12 A 2
Khanyiso 6 B 2
Kharkams 8 C 3
Khayakhulu 20 D 1
Khayamnandi 11 D 5
Khayelitsha 4 C 1
Khubvi 21 A 5
Khuis 16 C 1
Khukhune 12 A 2
Khuma 17 C 6
Khunotswane 17 A 5
Khureng 21 C 4
Khutsong 18 B 1
Khyayakhulu 17 A 6
Kidd's Beach 7 B 4
Kiepersol 19 A 4
Kiesel 20 C 2
Kieserville 17 B 5
Kilmun 12 B 3
Kimberley 11 A 4
Kinana 16 B 3
King William's Town 7 B 4
Kingsburgh 13 C 5
Kingscote 12 C 3
Kingsley 19 D 4
Kingswood 17 C 5
Kinkelbos 6 C 3
Kinross 18 B 2
Kirkwood 6 C 2
Klaarstroom 5 C 5
Klaserie 21 C 5
Klawer 4 A 1
Klein Bay 4 D 2
Klein Karas 14 D 3
Klein Sleutelfontein 5 B 5
Klein Tshipise 21 A 5
Kleinbegin 9 A 6
Kleinberg 5 D 5
Kleinemonde 7 C 4
Kleinmond 4 D 2
Kleinnood 20 C 3
Kleinplaat 5 C 5
Kleinpoort 6 C 2
Kleinsee 8 B 2
Klerksdorp 17 C 6
Klerkskraal 17 B 6
Klip River 18 B 1
Klipdale 4 D 3
Klipdam 15 C 5
Klipdrif 18 B 1
Klipfontein 12 B 1
Klipfontein 6 B 3
Klipplaat 6 B 1
Klipplaatdrift 17 B 6
Klippunt 10 A 1
Kliprand 9 C 4
Kliprivier 13 A 4
Klipskool 19 A 4
Klipwerf 9 D 5
Knapdaar 11 C 6
Kobe 9 D 4
Kochena 15 C 4
Koegasbrug 10 B 2
Koegrabie 10 A 1
Koekenaap 8 D 3
Koekoeskop 20 D 2
Koelemansrus 20 C 3
Koës 15 B 4
Koffiefontein 11 B 4
Koffiekraal 17 A 6

Kokerboom 15 D 5
Kokosi 18 B 1
Kokstad 12 C 3
Kokwaneng 21 A 4
Kolke 9 B 6
Kolo 12 B 1
Koloni 12 D 3
Komaggas 8 B 2
Komatipoort 19 A 5
Komga 7 B 5
Komkans 8 D 3
Komkhulu 7 A 5
Kommadagga 6 B 3
Kommandodrif 17 D 6
Kommetjie 4 D 1
Kommissiedrif 11 B 6
Kommissiepoort 12 B 1
Koningnaas 8 C 2
Konstabel 4 C 3
Koolbank 19 B 4
Koopan-Suid 15 C 6
Koopmansfontein Sta. 16 B 3
Koopmansfontein 10 A 3
Koornplaats 5 B 4
Kootjieskolk 9 D 5
Kopong 20 A 1
Koppies 18 C 1
Koringberg 4 B 1
Kosmos 18 A 1
Koster 17 B 6
Kotakata 17 C 6
Kotzeshoop 8 A 2
Kotzesrus 8 D 3
Koup 5 B 4
Koutjie 5 C 5
Kraaibrug 12 C 1
Kraaifontein 4 C 1
Kraaipan 17 B 5
Kraaldoom 5 C 4
Kraankuil 11 B 4
Krakeel River 5 C 6
Kransfontein 18 D 2
Kransfontein 19 B 4
Kranshoek 5 C 6
Kranskop 13 A 5
Kranspoort Dorp 18 A 3
Kromdraai 21 D 4
Kromellenboog 21 C 5
Kromrivier 5 A 6
Kromspruit 12 C 1
Kroomie 6 B 3
Kroondal 18 A 1
Kroonstad 18 D 1
Krugersdorp 18 B 1
Krugerspos 19 A 4
Kruidfontein 5 B 5
Kruis River 5 C 5
Kruisfontein 6 C 1
Kruispad 18 D 2
Kruispad 4 B 3
KuBhonxa 12 D 3
Kuboes 8 A 2
Kubusi 7 B 4
Kubuta 19 C 5
KuMaya 7 A 5
KuMbaxa 7 A 4
Kums 15 D 5
Ku-Ndeyingana 13 C 4
Kuruman 16 C 3
Kutenhuas 14 A 3
Kutlwano 11 A 4
Kutlwanong 17 D 6
Kuyasa 11 C 5
Kwa Magwaza 13 A 5
KwaBhubesi 12 C 2
KwaBityi 7 A 5
KwaDela 18 B 3
KwaDinda 12 D 3
KwaDukuza 13 B 5
KwaDungu 12 D 3
KwaFanti 7 A 4
Kwaggafontein 20 D 3
Kwaggaskloofdam 4 C 2
Kwa-Guqa 18 B 3
KwaJama 7 A 5
Kwakwatsi 18 C 1
KwaLupindo 12 C 2
KwaMadikana 7 A 4
KwaMafunze 13 B 4
KwaMahlathi 13 B 4
KwaMahomba 7 B 5
KwaMadlenkosi 5 A 5
KwaMakhutha 13 C 5
KwaMangati 7 A 4
KwaMashu 13 B 5
KwaMbonambi 13 A 6

PLACE NAMES INDEX

Name	Page	Name	Page	Name	Page	Name	Page	Name	Page	Name	Page	Name	Page	Name	Page
KwaMhlanga	18 A 2	Likhetlane	12 C 2	Mafukani	21 A 5	Maputo	19 B 6	Meadows	11 B 6	Mogologola	21 C 4	Mposa	13 A 6
Kwa-Mkhize	12 B 3	Limburg	20 B 3	Mafutseni	19 B 5	Maputsoe	12 A 2	Mecklenburg	21 C 4	Mogoto	21 C 4	Mpumalanga	19 D 5
KwaMpeko	7 C 4	Lime Acres	10 A 3	Magabeni	13 C 5	Maqabaqabeni	12 A 3	Mekaling	12 C 1	Mogwadi	21 B 4	Mpungamhlophe	19 D 5
KwaMzola	7 A 4	Linakeng	12 B 3	Magagane	21 B 6	Mara Sta.	21 B 4	Melinda	20 B 3	Mogwase	18 A 1	Mqanduli	7 A 5
KwaNdelane	7 A 5	Lindequesdrif	18 C 1	Magaliesburg	18 B 1	Mara	21 B 4	Melk River	20 C 3	Mohale's Hoek	12 C 1	Msikaba	12 D 3
KwaNgwanase	19 C 6	Lindeshof	4 D 2	Magatle	21 C 4	Maraisvlei	9 A 5	Melk	12 D 1	Mohlakeng	18 B 1	Mtati	7 C 4
KwaNobuhle	6 C 2	Lindley	18 D 1	Magdala	6 A 3	Marakabei	12 B 2	Melkbosstrand	4 C 1	Mohlaneng	18 B 1	Mthatha Mouth	7 A 6
KwaNojoli	6 B 2	Lindleyspoort	17 A 6	Magonya	21 B 5	Marakaneng	12 C 1	Melmoth	13 A 5	Mohlonong	20 C 3	Mthatha	7 A 6
KwaNokatana	7 A 5	Line Drift	7 B 4	Magoriapitse	17 A 5	Marambane	19 A 4	Meloding	17 D 6	Mokasa	17 D 4	Mtombeni	13 A 6
KwaNonzame	11 D 4	Linton	21 A 4	Magude	19 A 6	Marapyane	18 A 2	Meltonwold	10 D 2	Mokgalwaneng	20 D 1	Mtonjaneni	13 A 5
KwaNonzwakazi	6 C 3	Lionelton	18 B 2	Magudu	19 D 5	Marapyane	20 D 3	Melville	13 B 5	Mokgareng	17 D 4	Mtubatuba	13 A 6
KwaNtlola	12 C 3	Little Brak River	5 C 5	Mahalapye	20 B 1	Marble Hall	21 D 4	Memel	18 D 3	Mokgola	17 A 5	Mtunzini	13 A 5
KwaThandeka	19 C 4	Little Switzerland	12 A 3	Mahehle	13 C 4	Marburg	13 C 4	Meqheleng	12 A 1	Mokgomane	17 A 5	Mtwalume	13 C 4
Kwa-Thema	18 B 2	Lobamba	19 B 5	Mahetlwe	20 A 1	Marchand	9 A 5	Merriespruit	17 D 6	Mokgosi	20 A 1	Muden	13 A 4
KwaTinis	6 B 3	Lobatse	17 A 5	Mahlabatini	19 D 5	Mareetsane	17 B 5	Merriman	10 D 3	Mokhotlong	12 B 3	Muizenberg	4 C 1
KwaZamokuhle	18 B 3	Lochiel	19 B 4	Mahlangasi	19 D 5	Marite	21 D 5	Merrivale	13 B 4	Mokopane	20 C 3	Mukhomi	18 B 1
KwaZamukucinga	6 B 1	Loerie	6 C 2	Mahlatswetsa	12 A 1	Marken	20 B 3	Merry Pebble Stream		Mokopong	16 A 2	Muldersdrif	18 B 1
KwaZamuxolo	11 D 4	Loeriesfontein	9 D 4	Mahlutshini	12 B 3	Markramsdraai	16 D 2		21 D 6	Mokopung Ha Nkau	12 C 2	Munnik	21 B 4
KwaZanele	18 B 3	Logagane	17 B 4	Mahobong	12 A 2	Marlow	6 A 2	Merweville	5 B 4	Mokwalio	18 C 1	Munster	13 D 4
KwaZenzele	6 C 3	Logageng	17 A 4	Mahodi	21 B 4	Marnitz	20 B 3	Mesitsaneng	12 C 1	Molapole Maseko	18 A 1	Munyu	7 A 5
KwaZulu	7 A 6	Lohatla	16 D 2	Mahwelereng	20 C 3	Marobjan A	20 B 3	Messina	21 A 4	Molatedi	20 D 1	Murchison	21 C 5
Kwetyana	7 B 5	Lokweni	12 D 3	Maidstone	13 B 5	Marokolong	20 D 3	Metsimaholo	18 C 2	Molelema	17 D 4	Murraysburg	6 A 1
Kwezi	13 A 4	Longlands	11 A 4	Maile	18 A 1	Marquard	12 A 1	Meyerton	18 B 1	Molenrivier	5 C 5	Mushithe	21 A 4
		Longvue	6 C 3	Maipeing	17 B 5	Marracuene	19 A 6	Meyerville	18 C 3	Molepole	20 A 1	Musina	21 A 4
L		Lorraine	21 C 5	Maiphitlhwane	17 A 6	Marsala	18 D 2	Mgungundlovu	12 C 3	Molepolole	20 A 1	Muswodi	21 A 5
		Losdorings	17 D 6	Majwemasweu	11 A 6	Marulaneng	21 C 5	Mgwali	7 B 4	Moletsane	12 B 2	Mutale	21 A 5
L'Agulhas	4 D 3	Lose	20 B 1	Makapanstad	20 D 2	Marydale	10 B 2	Mgxojeni	12 C 3	Molimo Nthuse	12 B 2	Mvezo	7 A 5
La Cotte	21 B 5	Lotana	12 D 3	Makeleketla	12 A 1	Masakhane	12 D 1	Mhlambanyatsi	19 A 5	Molopo River	17 A 4	Mvumane	12 C 2
La Lucia	13 B 5	Lothair	19 B 4	Makgaung	21 C 5	Masakhe	11 D 6	Mhlambanyatsi	19 B 5	Moloto	20 D 3	Myfontein	10 D 3
La Mercy	13 B 5	Lotlhakane	17 B 5	Makgobistad	17 A 4	Masama	20 C 1	Mhlosheni	19 C 5	Molshoop	4 D 3	Mzamba Beach	13 D 4
Laaiplek	4 B 1	Loubad	20 C 3	Makgori	17 D 4	Maseru	12 B 1	Mhlume	19 B 5	Molteno	11 D 6	Mzamomhle	11 D 6
Ladismith	5 C 4	Louis Trichardt	21 B 4	Makhado	21 B 4	Mashaeng	12 A 2	Mhluzi	18 A 3	Molumong	12 B 3	Mzinti	19 A 5
Lady Frere	7 A 4	Louisvale	10 A 1	Makhwezini	13 A 6	Masham	12 C 1	Mica	21 C 5	Mononono	18 A 1	Mziwabantu	10 C 3
Lady Grey	12 C 1	Louisvale Road	9 A 6	Makobeng	20 B 2	Masibambane	12 D 2	Michausdal	6 A 2	Monontsha	12 A 2	
Ladybrand	12 B 1	Lourdes	12 C 3	Makokskraal	17 B 6	Masibekela	19 B 5	Mid Illovo	13 C 4	Mont Pelaan	18 D 3	**N**
Ladysmith	12 A 3	Lourensbeen	17 C 4	Makola	18 A 2	Masikhwa	21 A 5	Middel Koegas	10 B 2	Montagu	4 C 3	
Laersdrif	21 D 4	Louwna	17 C 4	Makonde	21 A 5	Masilo	12 A 1	Middelburg	11 D 4	Mont-aux-Sources	12 A 3	Nababeep	8 B 3
Lahlangubo	12 D 2	Louwsburg	19 D 5	Makopong	16 A 2	Masinda Lodge	13 A 6	Middelburg	18 A 3	Monte Christo	20 B 2	Nabas	15 D 5
Laing's Nek	18 C 3	Louwville	4 B 1	Makoppa	20 C 1	Masinyusane	10 D 3	Middeldrift	20 D 2	Montebello	13 B 5	Nabes	15 D 4
Laingsburg	5 B 4	Lower Blinkwater	6 B 3	Makoseni	13 A 5	Masisi	21 A 5	Middelfontein	20 C 3	Montrose	21 D 5	Nabies	15 D 4
Lakalakala	20 C 3	Loxton	10 D 2	Makubung	21 C 4	Masobe	18 A 2	Middelplaats Mine	16 C 2	Monyekeng	17 D 6	Naboomspruit	20 C 3
Lake Chrissie	19 B 4	Lubbeskolk	9 B 5	Makuleni	21 A 5	Massingir	21 B 6	Middelpos	4 A 3	Monzi	13 A 6	Nadi	13 A 4
Lake Eric	6 C 3	Lubhuku	19 B 5	Makwassie	17 C 5	Matableng	11 A 4	Middelrus	13 A 4	Mooi River	13 B 4	Nakop	15 D 5
Lambert's Bay	4 A 1	Luckhoff	11 B 4	Makwate	20 B 2	Matandele	19 C 5	Middleton	4 D 2	Mooifontein	14 B 2	Naledi	12 C 1
Lammerkop	21 D 4	Ludeke	12 D 3	Malaita	21 D 4	Matatiele	12 C 3	Middleton	6 B 3	Mooiplaas	7 B 5	Namaacha	19 B 5
Landplaas	8 D 3	Lukhanyisweni	11 C 4	Malapaneng	17 C 4	Matato	19 C 5	Middlewater	6 B 2	Mookane	20 B 1	Namahadi	18 C 2
Langberg	16 D 2	Lulekani	21 C 5	Malealea	12 B 1	Matebeng Ha Lelingoana		Midros	12 D 3	Mooketsi	21 B 4	Namakgale	21 C 5
Langebaan Road	4 B 1	Lundin's Nek	12 C 1	Malebogo	17 D 5		12 B 3	Miershoopholte	16 D 1	Moolman	19 C 4	Namies	9 B 4
Langebaan	4 B 1	Lundzi	19 B 4	Maleketla	21 B 5	Matelile	12 B 1	Migdol	17 C 5	Moorreesburg	4 B 1	Nanzes	15 D 4
Langholm	6 C 3	Lüneburg	19 C 4	Malelane Gate	21 D 6	Matenteng	20 D 3	Milford	19 D 4	Mopane	21 A 4	Napier	4 D 3
Langklip	15 D 6	Lunsklip	20 C 3	Maleshe	16 B 2	Mathathane	20 A 3	Miller	6 B 1	Morebeng	21 B 4	Nariep	8 C 3
Langkrans	19 D 4	Lusikisiki	12 D 3	Malgas	4 D 3	Mathopestad	18 B 1	Milnerton	4 C 1	Moretele	18 A 1	Narubis	15 C 4
Lavumisa	19 C 5	Lutsheko	7 A 6	Malingoaneng	12 B 3	Matiwane	13 A 4	Minera	18 C 3	Morgan's Bay	7 B 5	Natal Spa	19 D 4
Laxey	16 C 3	Luttig	5 B 5	Malkerns	19 B 5	Matjies River	5 C 5	Mirage	17 C 6	Morgenson	18 C 1	Nature's Valley	5 C 6
Leandra	18 B 2	Lutzburg	9 A 5	Malmesbury	4 C 1	Matjiesfontein	4 B 3	Misgund	5 C 6	Morgenzon	18 C 3	Ncwadi	13 B 4
Lebaneng	17 C 5	Lutzputs	9 A 5	Malomo	19 C 5	Matlabas	20 C 2	Mitchell's Plain	4 C 1	Morija	12 B 1	Ndabakazi	7 A 5
Lebogang	18 B 2	Lutzville	8 D 3	Malotwana	20 A 1	Matlakeng	12 C 1	Mjaliswa	12 D 3	Morojaneng	11 B 6	Ndakeni	12 D 3
Lebotloane	18 A 1	Luxeni	7 A 4	Malumelele	21 B 5	Matlala	20 D 3	Mjanyana	7 A 5	Morokwaneng	16 B 3	Ndaleni	13 B 4
Lebowakgomo	21 C 4	Luyengo	19 B 5	Mamafubedu	18 D 2	Matlerekeng	20 D 3	Mjula	7 A 5	Morokweng	16 B 3	Ndevana	7 B 4
Ledig	20 D 1	Lydenburg	21 D 5	Mamaila	21 B 5	Matloding	17 B 4	Mkambati	13 D 4	Morone	21 D 5	NdlunKulu	7 A 5
Leeudoringstad	17 C 6	Lykso	16 C 3	Mamathwane	16 C 2	Matlomola	10 A 3	Mkhazane	13 A 5	Morristown	12 D 1	Ndumo	19 C 6
Leeufontein	18 A 2			Mamelodi	18 A 2	Matlope	20 B 2	Mkhuhlu	21 D 6	Mortimer	6 A 2	Ndundulu	13 A 5
Leeu-Gamka	5 B 5	**M**		Mammutla	17 D 4	Matlwangtlwang	18 D 1	Mkhulu	19 A 5	Morupule	20 A 1	Ndwedwe	13 B 5
Leeupoort	20 D 2			Mamre	4 C 1	Matola	19 B 6	Mkondeni	13 B 4	Moses Mabida	6 C 2	Ndzingeni	19 B 5
Legkraal	21 B 4	Maake	21 C 5	Manamakgoteng	20 D 2	Matoporong	11 B 6	Mkukwini	12 A 3	Mosesh's Ford	12 C 2	Neilersdrif	9 A 6
Legonyane	20 D 2	Maanhaarrand	18 B 1	Manchabeni	21 C 5	Matroosberg	4 C 3	Mkuze	19 D 5	Mosita	17 B 4	Neisip	14 B 2
Lehurutshe	17 A 5	Maartenshoop	19 A 4	Mandala	21 A 5	Matsa	21 A 4	Mlamu	19 A 5	Mosomane	20 C 1	Nekina	12 D 2
Leipoldtville	4 A 1	Maasstroom	20 A 3	Mandini	13 B 5	Matsap	10 A 2	Mliba	19 B 5	Mossel Bay	5 D 5	Nelsdrif	17 D 6
Lejone	12 B 2	Mabaalstad	17 A 6	Mandluntsha	7 A 5	Matsapha	19 B 5	Mmakgori	17 B 4	Motetema	21 D 4	Nelshoogte	19 B 4
Lekgophung	20 A 1	Mabede	12 D 3	Mangaung	11 B 6	Matsha	12 D 3	Mmamabula	20 B 1	Moteti	20 D 3	Nelspoort	5 A 6
Lekkersing	8 A 2	Mabehana	7 A 6	Mangeni	12 D 3	Matshona	12 D 3	Mmamahabane	18 D 1	Mothibistad	16 C 3	Nelspruit	21 D 5
Lekoko	17 B 5	Mabeskraal	17 A 6	Mangobomvu	7 A 5	Matsieng	12 B 1	Mmamatlakala	20 C 3	Motjane	19 B 4	Netherby	12 B 3
Lekokoaneng	12 B 1	Mabibi	19 C 6	Mangoloaneng	12 C 2	Matsulu	19 A 5	Mmanethlake	18 A 2	Motlhabe	17 A 6	Nevada	12 B 1
Leliefontein	8 C 3	Maboloko	18 A 1	Mangwane	7 A 5	Matukeng	12 B 1	Mmankgodi	20 A 1	Motlhabeng	17 B 5	New Amalfi	12 C 3
Lemoenshoek	5 C 4	Mabopane	18 A 1	Mangwaneni	12 A 3	Matwabeng	12 A 1	Mmatau	17 A 6	Motlolo	21 C 5	New England	12 C 2
Lenasia	18 B 1	Mabula	20 D 2	Mangwaneni	12 D 3	Maunatlala	20 A 2	Mmathethe	17 A 6	Motsekuoa	12 B 1	New Hanover	13 B 4
Lengelihle	6 A 2	Mabule	17 A 4	Manhiça	19 A 6	Mautse	12 A 2	Mmopyane	17 A 6	Motsweding	17 D 4	New Largo	18 B 2
Lennoxton	18 D 3	Mabvuka Jazz	21 A 4	Mankayane	19 C 4	Mavhulani	21 B 5	Mnyani	17 C 4	Mount Alida	13 B 5	New Machavie	17 C 6
Lentsweletau	20 A 1	Macaene	21 D 6	Mankweng	21 C 4	Mayireni	7 A 4	Mnyani	17 C 4	Mount Ayliff	12 D 3	Newcastle	18 D 3
Lephalale	20 B 2	Macene	21 B 5	Mannamead	21 B 4	Mazenod	12 B 1	Moamba	19 A 6	Mount Carmel	16 D 3	Newington	21 D 6
Lepho	11 C 5	Machadodorp	19 A 4	Mansfield	17 B 4	Mazeppa Bay	7 B 5	Mochudi	20 A 1	Mount Elias	13 B 5	Newtown	9 D 5
Lerala	20 A 2	Machaneng	20 B 2	Manthestad	17 D 4	Mazista	17 A 6	Modder River	11 A 4	Mount Fletcher	12 C 2	Ngagane	18 D 3
Lesseyton	7 A 4	Machangulo	19 B 6	Mantsho	20 D 1	Mbabane	19 B 5	Modimolle	20 C 3	Mount Frere	12 D 3	Ngangelizwe	12 D 2
Letaba	21 C 5	Macia	19 A 6	Mantsonyane	12 B 2	Mbalakweza	7 A 4	Modimong	20 D 1	Mount Moorosi	12 C 2	Ngcabasa	7 B 4
Letjiesbos	5 B 5	Macleantown	7 B 4	Manubi	7 B 5	Mbashe	7 A 5	Modipane	20 A 1	Mount Stewart	6 B 1	Ngcobo	7 A 5
Letlhabile	18 A 1	Maclear	12 D 2	Manyana	20 A 1	Mbazwana	19 C 6	Modjadjiskloof	21 B 4	Moyeni (Quthing)	12 C 1	Ngobi	20 D 2
Letshana	20 A 2	Madadeni	18 D 3	Manyano	12 D 1	Mbhawula	21 B 5	Modutung	17 D 4	Mpafane	12 D 2	Ngodwana	21 D 5
Letsitele	21 C 5	Madadeni	19 B 5	Manyatseng	12 A 2	Mbhongo	18 A 2	Moebani	19 B 4	Mpaka	19 B 5	Ngomane	19 B 5
Letswatla	20 B 3	Madibogo	17 B 5	Manzi	7 A 6	Mbongweni	12 C 3	Moedig	19 B 4	Mpekweni	6 C 3	Ngome	19 D 5
Levubu	21 C 5	Madietane	20 D 3	Manzini	19 B 5	Mbulungwane	19 C 5	Moedwil	17 A 6	Mpemvana	19 D 4	Ngqeleni	7 A 6
Leybank	15 A 4	Madikgetla	11 C 5	Maokeng	18 D 1	McCarthy's Rest	16 B 2	Moemaneng	12 A 1	Mpetha	7 B 5	Ngubevu	13 A 4
Leydsdorp	21 C 5	Madipelesa	17 D 4	Mapai	21 A 6	McGregor	4 C 3	Moeng	20 A 2	Mphahlele	21 C 4	Ngwathe	18 D 1
Libertas	18 D 1	Madombidzha	21 B 4	Maphalong	21 C 4	Mdantsane	7 B 4	Moeswal	16 D 2	Mphakane	21 B 4	Ngwenya	19 B 4
Libode	12 D 3	Mafahaneng	18 D 2	Maphodi	11 C 5	Mbongo	18 A 2	Mofutshepe	11 C 6	Mphaki	12 C 2	Ngwenyeni	19 A 5
Lichtenburg	17 B 5	Mafeteng	12 B 1	Mapholaneng	12 B 3	Mbongweni	12 C 3	Mogapi	20 A 2	Mphelelo	20 B 3	Ngxanga	12 D 3
Lidgetton	13 B 4	Mafikeng	17 B 5	Mapoleseng	12 C 2	Mbulungwane	19 C 5	Mogapinyana	20 A 2	Mpheleng	20 D 3	Nhlangano	19 B 5
Likalaneng	12 B 2	Mafube	12 C 2	Mapoteng	12 A 2	McGregor	4 C 3	Mogoditshane	20 A 1	Mpila Lodge	13 A 6	Nhlazatje	19 B 4
				Mapulanguene	21 C 6	Mdantsane	7 B 4	Mogodishane	20 A 1	Mpolweni	13 B 4	Nhlazatshe	19 D 5

Name	Page		Name	Page
Niekerkshoop	10 B 2		Olyfberg	21 B 4
Nietverdiend	17 A 5		Omdraaisvlei	10 C 3
Nieu-Bethesda	6 A 1		Onder-Wadrif	4 A 3
Nieuwoudtville	9 D 4		Ongers	10 C 3
Nigel	18 B 2		Onrus River	4 D 2
Nigramoep	8 B 2		Onseepkans	9 A 4
Nissenville	5 C 4		Oorlogspoort	11 D 5
Nkande	19 D 4		Op die Berg	4 B 2
Nkandla	13 A 5		Opperman	11 B 4
Nkanyezi	13 A 4		Opuzane	19 C 4
Nkonjane	13 A 6		Orange River	11 B 4
Nkqubela	4 C 3		Orangeville	18 C 2
Nkululeko	12 D 1		Orania	11 B 4
Nkumandeni	7 A 6		Oranjemund	8 A 1
Nkumba	13 B 4		Oranjevallei	10 A 1
Nkungwini	12 D 3		Orkney	17 C 6
Nkwalini	13 A 5		Orpen Gate	21 C 6
Nkwe	20 B 3		oSizweni	19 D 4
Nkwenkwezi	7 C 4		Otimati	13 B 5
Nobumba	7 C 4		Otse	17 A 5
Nocwane	7 A 5		Ottosdal	17 C 5
Noenieput	15 D 5		Ottoshoop	17 A 5
Noetzie	5 C 6		Oudekraalfontein	4 B 1
Nokaneng	18 A 2		Oudtshoorn	5 C 5
Nolukhanyo	7 C 4		Ouhoutdraai	18 C 2
Nomathamsanga	6 C 2		Oukraal	4 D 2
Nomonde	11 D 6		Ouplaas	4 D 3
Nompumelelo	11 D 4		Oven	5 B 6
Nondweni	19 D 4		Overwacht	20 B 2
Nongoma	19 D 5		Overyssel	20 B 3
Nonzwakazi	10 C 3		Oviston	11 C 5
Nooitgedacht	11 A 4		Owen's Cutting	13 A 5
Nooitgedacht	5 C 5		Owendale	16 D 3
Nooitgedacht	17 B 5		Oxbow	12 A 2
Noordhoek	4 C 1		Oyster Bay	6 D 1
Noordkaap	19 A 4			
Noordoewer	8 A 2		**P**	
Normandien	18 D 3		Paarl	4 C 2
Northam	20 D 2		Paballelo	10 A 1
Norvalspont	11 C 5		Pachsdraai	17 A 6
Nossob Lodge	15 A 6		Paddock	13 C 4
Notintsila	7 A 6		Paddon	16 A 3
Nottingham Road	13 B 4		Padstow	16 C 3
Noupoort	11 D 4		Pafuri Gate	21 A 5
Nous	9 A 5		Palala	20 C 3
Nozizwe	11 D 5		Palapye	20 A 1
Nqabeni	13 C 4		Paleisheuwel	4 B 1
Nqalweni	12 C 3		Palm Beach	13 D 4
Nqutu	19 D 4		Palmerton	12 D 3
Nseleni	13 A 6		Palmietfontein	17 C 5
Nshongweni	13 B 4		Pampierstad	17 D 4
Nsikazi	19 A 4		Pampoenpoort	10 D 2
Nsoko	19 C 5		Panbult	19 C 4
Ntabankulu	12 D 3		Papendorp	4 A 1
Ntambanana	13 A 5		Papkuil	10 A 3
Ntha	18 D 1		Paradise Beach	6 C 2
Nthorwane	18 C 2		Paradise	17 C 4
Ntibane	7 A 6		Park Rynie	13 C 4
Ntlhantlhe	20 A 1		Parow	4 C 1
Ntlhaveni	21 A 5		Parr's Halt	20 B 2
Ntselamanzi	7 B 4		Parys	18 C 1
Ntsundwane	7 A 6		Patensie	6 C 2
Ntunjambili	13 A 5		Paternoster	4 B 1
Ntwane	21 D 4		Paterson	6 C 3
Ntywenka	12 D 2		Paul Kruger Gate	21 D 6
Numbi Gate	21 D 6		Paul Roux	18 D 1
Nutfield	20 D 3		Paulpietersburg	19 C 4
Nuwefontein	15 D 4		Peace Town	12 A 3
Nuwerus	8 D 3		Pearly Beach	4 D 2
Nuy	4 C 2		Pearson's Hunt	16 D 1
Nxaxo Mouth	7 B 5		Pearston	6 B 2
Nyalasa	7 A 4		Peddie	7 B 4
Nyalazi River	19 D 6		Peka	12 A 2
Nyandeni	12 D 3		Pelindaba	18 B 1
Nyanyadu	19 D 4		Pella	17 A 6
Nyarha	6 B 3		Pella	9 A 4
Nyezane	13 A 5		Penge	21 C 5
Nylstroom	20 C 3		Pennington	13 C 4
Nyongwana	7 A 4		Penryn	16 C 2
Nyoni	13 A 5		Pepworth	13 A 4
Nzhelele	21 A 4		Perdeberg	11 A 5
Nzwakazi	7 A 6		Perdekop	18 C 3
			Persip	15 A 4
O			Perth	16 B 2
Oatlands	6 B 1		Petersburg	6 A 2
Oberholzer	18 B 1		Petrus Steyn	18 D 2
Obobogorob	15 C 5		Petrusburg	11 B 5
Odendaalsrus	17 D 6		Petrusville	11 C 5
Oetting	13 C 4		Petsana	18 D 2
Ofcolaco	21 C 5		Pevensey	12 B 3
Ogies	18 B 2		Pfolz	14 B 3
Ohrigstad	21 D 5		Phahameng	11 A 6
Okiep	8 B 3		Phahameng	20 C 3
Old Bunting	7 A 6		Phalaborwa Gate	21 C 6
Old Morley	7 A 6		Phalaborwa	21 C 5
Olifants Drift	20 C 1		Phamong	12 C 2
Olifantshoek	16 D 2		Phathakahle	17 D 6

Name	Page		Name	Page
Phelandaba	19 C 6		Queensberry Bay	7 B 5
Phelindaba	10 A 3		Queensburgh	13 B 5
Phepheng	16 A 2		Queenstown	7 A 4
Philadelphia	4 C 1		Quiba	12 D 2
Philippolis	11 C 5		Quiing	12 B 1
Philipstown	11 C 4		Qumbu	12 D 3
Phiritona	18 C 1		Qumra	7 B 5
Phoenix	18 B 3		Qunu	7 A 5
Phokeng	18 A 1			
Phokwane	21 D 4		**R**	
Phola	18 B 2		Radisele	20 A 1
Phomolong	17 D 6		Raditshaba	20 A 3
Phomolong	18 D 2		Radium	20 D 3
Phuthaditjhaba	12 A 3		Railton	4 C 3
Pienaar's River	20 D 3		Ramabanta	12 B 2
Piet Plessis	17 B 4		Ramatlabama	17 A 5
Piet Retief	19 C 4		Rammulotsi	17 C 6
Pietermaritzburg	13 B 4		Ramohlakoana	12 C 3
Pietersburg	21 C 4		Ramokgonami	20 A 2
Piggs Peak	19 B 5		Ramokokastad	18 A 1
Pigott's Bridge	6 B 3		Ramotswa	20 A 1
Piketberg	4 B 1		Ramsgate	13 D 4
Pilgrim's Rest	19 A 4		Randburg	18 B 1
Pilikwe	20 A 2		Randfontein	18 B 1
Pinetown	13 B 5		Rankin's Pass	20 C 2
Pitseng	12 A 2		Rantebeng	20 D 2
Pitsi's Nek	12 A 2		Raphahlelo	21 B 4
Pitsimatome	20 B 3		Rapitsi	20 D 2
Platbakkies	8 C 3		Rasesa	20 A 1
Platjan	20 A 3		Ratanang	11 B 4
Platkoppiesdrif	12 D 1		Ratanda	18 B 2
Platrand	18 C 3		Ratelfontein	4 A 1
Plettenberg Bay	5 C 6		Rawsonville	4 C 2
Plooysburg	11 A 4		Rayton	18 A 2
Poding-tse-Rolo	11 C 5		Reagile	17 B 6
Pofadder	9 B 4		Rebone	20 B 3
Politsi	21 B 4		Reddersburg	11 B 6
Polokwane	21 C 4		Redelinghuys	4 B 1
Pomeroy	13 A 4		Redhouse	6 C 2
Pomfret	16 B 3		Redlands	10 B 2
Pomona	14 C 1		Redoubt	13 D 4
Ponta do Ouro	19 C 6		Reedstream Park	18 B 3
Pontdrif	20 A 3		Refengkgotso	18 C 1
Pools	4 B 2		Regina	17 C 6
Port Alfred	7 C 4		Reitz	18 D 2
Port Beaufort	4 D 3		Reivilo	17 A 4
Port Durnford	13 A 6		Renosterkop	5 A 6
Port Edward	13 D 4		Rensburgdorp	18 B 2
Port Grosvenor	13 D 4		Ressano Garcia	21 D 6
Port Henrique	19 B 6		Retanda	18 B 2
Port Nolloth	8 B 2		Rhadhopololo	20 A 3
Port Shepstone	13 C 4		Rhenospruit	17 C 6
Port St Johns	12 D 3		Rhodes	12 D 2
Porterville	4 B 2		Richards Bay	13 A 6
Post Chalmers	6 A 2		Richmond	10 D 3
Postmasburg	10 A 3		Richmond	13 B 4
Potchefstroom	18 C 1		Riebeeck-East	6 B 3
Potfontein	11 C 4		Riebeeckstad	17 D 6
Potgietersrus	20 C 3		Riebeek West	4 C 2
Poupan	11 C 4		Riebeek-Kasteel	4 C 2
Pretoria North	18 A 2		Riemvasmaak	9 A 5
Pretoria	18 A 2		Rietbron	5 B 6
Prieska	10 C 3		Rietfontein	15 C 5
Prince Albert Road	5 B 4		Rietfontein	21 C 5
Prince Albert	5 B 5		Rietkuil	18 B 3
Prince Alfred Hamlet	4 C 2		Rietpan	17 C 5
Pringle Bay	4 D 2		Rietpoel	4 D 2
Priors	11 C 5		Rietpoort	8 D 3
Protem	4 D 3		Rietspruit	12 A 1
Protest	19 C 4		Rietvlei	13 C 4
Providence	11 C 5		Ringane	21 C 6
Pudimoe	17 C 4		Rini	6 C 3
Pudumong	17 C 4		Ritchie	11 A 4
Pullen's Hope	18 B 1		Rite	21 D 4
Punda Maria Gate	21 A 5		River View	13 A 6
Putsonderwater	10 B 1		Riversdale	18 B 1
Pyramid	18 A 2		Riversdale	5 C 4
			Riverside	12 C 3
Q			Riverton	11 A 4
Qaba	12 B 1		Riviersonderend	4 D 3
Qacha's Nek	12 C 2		Roadside	18 B 2
Qalabotjha	18 C 2		Robben Island	4 C 1
Qalo	12 A 2		Roberts Drift	18 C 2
Qaqane	12 D 1		Robertson	4 C 3
Qarnata	7 A 4		Roedtan	20 C 3
Qawukeni	7 B 4		Roleleothunya	11 C 6
Qedusizi	19 D 4		Rolle	21 D 6
Qhalasi	12 C 1		Roma	12 B 2
Qibing	11 B 6		Roodepan	11 B 4
Qobong Ha Tsiu	12 C 1		Roodepoort	18 B 1
Qokama	7 A 5		Roodewal	19 B 4
Qolora Mouth	7 B 5		Rooiberg	20 D 2
Qomoqomong	12 C 1		Rooibokkraal	20 C 1
Qora Mouth	7 B 5		Rooibosbult	20 C 2
Qota	7 A 5		Rooiels	4 D 2
Qudeni	13 A 5		Rooifontein	8 C 3
			Rooigrond	17 B 5

Name	Page		Name	Page
Rooihoogte	6 A 2		Sehonghong	12 B 3
Rooikraal	18 C 1		Sekake	12 C 2
Rooikraal	21 D 4		Sekhing	17 D 4
Rooilyf	10 A 1		Sekhukhune	21 D 4
Rooirivier	5 C 5		Sekwati	21 C 5
Rooiwal	18 C 1		Selatirivier	21 C 5
Rookdale	12 A 3		Seleka	20 A 2
Roosboom	12 A 3		Selokolela	17 A 4
Roossenekal	21 D 4		Selonsrivier	21 D 4
Rorke's Drift	13 A 4		Semonkong	12 B 2
Rosebank	13 B 4		Sendelingsdrif	14 D 2
Rosedene	5 A 5		Sendelingsplaas	20 D 1
Rosehaugh	19 A 4		Senekal	18 D 1
Rosendal	12 A 2		Senlac	16 B 3
Rosetta	13 B 4		Senotlelo	20 D 3
Rosh Pinah	14 D 2		Sentrum	20 C 2
Rosmead	11 D 5		Senwabarwana	20 B 3
Ross Mission	12 C 2		Seoding	16 C 3
Rossouw	12 D 1		Sephaku	18 A 3
Rothe	12 B 1		Sepharane	20 C 3
Rotkop	14 C 1		Seqalem	12 A 3
Rouxpos	5 C 4		Serake	17 A 5
Rouxville	12 C 1		Seretse	11 A 5
Royal Kraal	19 D 5		Serfontein	18 C 1
Rugseer	10 B 1		Seru	7 A 5
Ruitersbos	5 C 5		Sesehu	21 C 4
Rusplaas	21 D 5		Seshego	21 C 4
Rust	4 C 1		Seshote	12 B 2
Rustenburg	18 A 1		Sesobe	20 D 1
Rustfontein	12 C 3		Setlagole	17 B 4
Rustig	18 C 1		Settlers	20 D 3
Rusverby	20 D 1		Seven Fountains	6 C 3
Ryno	12 D 2		Seven Oaks	13 B 4
			Severn	16 B 2
S			Seymour	7 B 4
Saaibult	12 A 1		Sezela	13 C 4
Saaifontein	5 A 5		Shaka's Rock	13 B 5
Sabelo	10 D 3		Shakaskraal	13 B 5
Sabie	21 D 5		Shakung	20 D 2
Sada	7 A 4		Shannon	11 B 6
Saggiesberg	9 D 4		Sharpeville	18 C 1
Sakhile	18 C 3		Shaw Park	7 C 4
Sakrivier	9 D 5		Shayandima	21 B 5
Salamanga	19 B 6		Sheepmoor	19 C 4
Saldanha	4 B 1		Sheffield Beach	13 B 5
Salem	6 C 3		Shelly Beach	13 D 4
Salitje	19 C 5		Sherborne	11 D 4
Salpeterpan	17 C 4		Sheridan	12 A 2
Salt Lake	10 B 3		Sherwood	20 A 2
Salt Rock	13 B 5		Shigalo	21 A 5
Sand Bay	4 D 2		Shirley	15 B 4
Sandberg	4 A 1		Shongoane	20 B 2
Sandfontein	18 A 1		Sibasa	21 A 5
Sandlane	19 B 4		Sicunusa	19 C 4
Sandspruit	18 C 3		Sidbury	6 C 3
Sandton	18 B 1		Sidvokodvo	19 B 5
Sandverhaar	14 C 3		Sidwadweni	12 D 3
Sandvlakte	6 C 1		Sigangeni	19 B 4
Sani Pass	12 B 3		Signalberg	14 D 3
Sannaspos	11 B 6		Sigundwaneni	12 D 3
Sannieshof	17 B 5		Sihhoye	19 B 5
Santa Maria	19 B 6		Sihlabeni	7 A 5
Sasolburg	18 C 1		Sijungqwini	7 A 6
Satco	15 D 4		Sikobeni	7 A 5
Sauer	4 B 1		Silaka	7 A 6
Saulspoort	18 A 1		Silent Valley	20 C 1
Scarborough	4 D 1		Silkaatskop	20 D 1
Schlechtgenoeg	6 A 2		Silobela	19 B 4
Schmidtsdrif	10 A 3		Siloe	12 C 1
Schoemanshoek	5 C 5		Silutshana	13 A 5
Schoemansville	18 A 1		Silver Streams	10 A 3
Scholtz	5 C 5		Silwerkrans	17 A 6
Schoombee	11 D 5		Simlangetja	19 C 4
Schoongelegen	20 A 3		Simon's Town	4 D 1
Schoongezicht	6 B 3		Simuma	13 C 4
Schwarzkuppe	14 A 2		Simunye	19 B 5
Schweizer-Reneke	17 C 5		Sinakho	11 D 6
Scottburgh	13 C 5		Sinakho	12 D 1
Sea Park	13 C 4		Siphofaneni	19 C 5
Sea View	6 C 2		Sir Lowry's Pass	4 D 2
Sebapala	12 C 2		Sishen Mine	16 D 2
Seboche	12 A 2		Sishen	16 D 2
Sebokeng	18 B 1		Siteki	19 B 5
Sefare	20 B 2		Sithobela	19 C 5
Sefikeng	12 B 2		Sittingbourne	7 B 4
Sefophe	20 A 2		Sivukile	18 C 3
Seforong	12 C 2		Siyabuswa	20 D 3
Segole	20 B 3		Siyathemba	18 C 2
Sehlabathebe	12 C 2		Siyathuthuka	18 A 3
Sehlakwane	18 A 3		Sizamela	5 D 4
			Sizanani Village	18 A 2

Name	Page
Skoonspruit	17 D 6
Skuinsdrif	20 D 1
Skukuza	21 D 6
Slabberts	12 A 2
Slangfontein	5 A 5
Slangrivier	5 D 4
Slurry	17 B 5
Smithfield	11 C 6
Smitskraal	6 C 1
Sneeukraal	5 A 5
Sobabili	12 A 3
Sodium	10 C 3
Soebatsfontein	8 C 2
Soekmekaar	21 B 4
Somerset East	6 B 2
Somerset West	4 C 2
Somerset	20 C 1
Sondagsloop	20 C 3
Sonop	11 B 6
Sonop	18 A 1
Sonskyn	11 C 6
Sonstraal	16 C 2
Sorgvliet	11 B 5
Soshanguve	20 D 2
Sotong	21 B 5
Soutfontein	8 C 2
Southbroom	13 D 4
Southey	16 C 3
Southport	13 C 4
Southwell	6 C 3
Soutkuil	4 B 1
Soutpan	11 A 5
Soweto	18 B 1
Spanwerk	20 C 1
Speelmanskraal	5 C 6
Spes Bona	14 A 1
Spitskopvlei	6 A 2
Spoegrivier	8 C 3
Spring Valley	6 A 3
Springbok	8 B 3
Springfontein	11 C 5
Springs	18 B 2
Spytfontein	11 A 4
St Faith's	13 C 4
St George's Strand	6 C 2
St Helena Bay	4 B 1
St Lucia Estuary	13 A 6
St Mark's	7 A 4
St Matthews	19 D 4
Stafford's Post	12 C 3
Standerton	18 C 3
Stanford	4 D 2
Stanford's Cove	4 D 2
Steel's Drift	18 C 3
Steelpoort	21 D 5
Steenbokpan	20 B 2
Steilloopbrug	20 B 3
Steinkop	8 B 3
Stella	17 B 4
Stellenbosch	4 C 2
Sterkrivier	20 C 3
Sterkspruit	12 C 1
Sterkstroom	11 D 4
Sterling	10 D 1
Steynsburg	11 D 5
Steynsrus	18 D 1
Steynville	11 B 4
Steytlerville	6 C 1
Stilfontein	17 C 6
Still Bay	5 D 4
Stockpoort	20 B 2
Stoffberg	21 D 4
Stofvlei	9 C 4
Stompneus Bay	4 B 1
Stormberg	11 D 6
Storms River Mouth	6 C 1
Storms River	6 C 1
Stormsvlei	4 C 3
Straatsdrif	20 D 1
Strand	4 C 2
Strandfontein	4 A 1
Straussburg	10 A 1
Struis Bay	4 D 3
Strydenburg	10 C 3
Strydomsvlei	5 B 6
Strydpoort	17 C 5
Studtis	6 C 1
Stutterheim	7 B 4
Süderecke	14 A 2
Sukkelaar	18 B 3
Sulenkama	12 D 2
Summerstrand	6 C 2
Sundra	18 B 2
Sundumbili	13 B 5
Sunland	6 C 2
Susannahspos	12 A 1
Susannaskop	18 D 2

PLACE NAMES INDEX

	Page			Page			Page			Page			Page
Sutherland	4 A 3	Tlhabologang	17 B 6	Umkomaas	13 C 5	Vouga	21 A 6	Witpan	10 A 2
Sutton	16 C 2	Tlhakgameng	17 B 4	Umlazi	13 C 5	Vrede	18 C 3	Witpoort	17 C 5
Suurberg	6 C 2	Tlholong	12 A 2	Umphumulo	13 B 5	Vredefort	18 C 1	Witput	11 B 4
Suurbraak	4 C 3	Tlokoeng	12 B 3	Umtentweni	13 C 4	Vredenburg	4 B 1	Witpütz	14 D 2
Swartberg	12 C 3	Toeslaan	9 A 5	uMunywana	13 A 5	Vredendal	4 A 1	Witrand	18 B 3
Swartkop	10 C 1	Togo	6 C 2	Umzamomhle	6 C 2	Vredeshoop	15 C 5	Witrandsfontein	17 B 6
Swartkops	6 C 2	Toleni Head	7 A 5	uMzimkulu	13 C 4	Vroenspan	15 D 6	Wittenberg	19 C 4
Swart-Mfolozi	19 D 5	Tolwe	20 B 3	uMzinto	13 C 4	Vryburg	17 C 4	Witwater	4 B 1
Swartmodder	15 D 6	Tom Burke	20 B 2	uMzumbe	13 C 4	Vryheid	19 D 4	Witwater	8 C 3
Swartputs	16 D 3	Tongaat Beach	13 B 5	Underberg	12 B 3	Vukusakhe	18 C 3	Wolmaransstad	17 C 5
Swartruggens	17 A 6	Tongaat	13 B 5	Uniondale	5 C 6	Vuwani	21 B 5	Wolplaas	15 D 4
Swartwater	20 A 3	Tontelbos	9 D 5	Upington	10 A 1	Vuyolwethu	6 C 1	Wolseley	4 C 2
Swawel	9 D 5	Tooseng	21 C 4	Upper Chilton	7 A 4	Vyandsvlei	18 C 1	Wolwefontein	5 C 4
Swellendam	4 C 3	Tosca	16 B 3	Upper Telle	12 C 1	Vyeboom	21 B 5	Wolwefontein	6 C 2
Swempoort	12 D 1	Touws River	4 C 3	Urionskraal	4 A 2	Vyeboom	4 C 2	Wolwehoek	18 C 1
Swinburne	12 A 3	Toyise	7 B 4	Urionskraal	9 D 4			Wolwespruit	11 A 5
Sydney on Vaal	11 A 4	Trawal	4 A 1	Usutu	20 A 3	**W**		Wonderfontein	18 B 3
Syferfontein	17 B 6	Treves	20 B 3	Utlwanang	17 D 4			Wonderheuwel	18 C 1
Syfergat	11 D 6	Trichardt	18 B 3	Utrecht	19 D 4	Waenhuiskrans (Arniston)	4 D 3	Wonderkop	18 D 1
		Trichardtsdal	21 C 5	Uvongo	13 D 4	Wag 'n Bietjie	19 C 4	Wondermere	17 A 6
T		Trompsburg	11 C 5			Wagenaarskraal	5 A 5	Wongalethu	6 B 1
		Trooilapspan	10 A 1	**V**		Wakefield	18 B 2	Woodbine	20 D 1
Taaiboschgroet	20 A 3	Tsakane	18 B 2			Wakkerstroom	19 C 4	Woodford	12 A 3
Tabankulu	12 D 3	Tsa-Kholo	12 B 1	Vaal Gamagara	11 A 4	Walkerville	18 B 1	Woodlands	6 C 1
Table Mountain	13 B 4	Tsatsane	21 C 4	Vaal Marina	18 C 2	Wallekraal	8 C 2	Woodlands	7 B 4
Table View	4 C 1	Tsatsaneng	21 C 4	Vaalboshoek	17 D 4	Wanda	11 B 4	Worcester	4 C 2
Tafelberg	11 D 5	Tsaukaib	14 C 1	Vaalhoek	21 D 5	Waqu	7 A 4	Wrenchville	16 C 3
Takazi	7 B 5	Tsawisis	14 B 3	Vaalplaats	17 B 5	Warburton	19 B 4	Wuppertal	4 A 2
Tamasane	20 A 2	Tses	14 B 3	Vaalwater	20 C 2	Warden	18 D 2	Wurasoord	11 B 5
Tarka Bridge	6 A 2	Tsetsebjwe	20 A 3	Val	18 C 2	Warmbad Noord	9 A 4		
Tarkastad	6 A 3	Tshabong	16 B 2	Valspan	17 D 4	Warmbad	9 A 4	**X**	
Taung	17 D 4	Tshakhuma	21 B 5	Valsrivier	18 D 2	Warmbaths	20 D 3		
Taupye	20 A 2	Tshamahansi	20 C 3	Van Dyks	18 B 3	Warmfontein	15 C 4	Xalanga	12 D 1
Tebellong	12 C 2	Tshaneni	19 B 5	Van Reenen	12 A 3	Warmwaterberg	5 C 4	Xawela	21 B 5
Teebus	11 D 5	Tshani	7 A 6	Van Stadens	6 C 2	Warrenton	17 D 4	Xinavane	19 A 6
Tele Bridge	12 C 1	Tshatshu	7 A 4	Van Stadensrus	12 C 1	Wartburg	13 B 4	Xolobe	7 A 4
Temba	20 D 3	Tshepong	11 A 6	Van Wyksdorp	5 C 4	Wasbank	19 D 4		
Tembinkosi	11 C 4	Tshiame	12 A 3	Van Wyksrus	17 C 6	Wasser	14 B 3	**Y**	
Tembisa	18 B 2	Tshidilamolomo	17 B 6	Van Wyksvlei	10 C 1	Waterford	6 B 2		
Terra Firma	16 A 3	Tshing	17 B 6	Van Zylsrus	16 C 1	Waterkloof	11 C 5	York	13 B 4
Tevoit	6 A 2	Tshiozwi	21 B 4	Vanderbijlpark	18 C 1	Waterpoort	21 A 4	Ypres	20 C 3
Teyateyaneng	12 B 1	Tshipise	21 A 5	Vanderkloof	11 C 4	Watersend	16 A 2	Yzerfontein	4 C 1
Teza	13 A 6	Tsilwana	16 B 3	Vanrhynsdorp	4 A 1	Waterval Boven	19 A 4		
Thaba Bosiu	12 B 1	Tsineng	16 C 2	Vant's Drift	19 D 4	Waterval Onder	19 A 4	**Z**	
Thaba Nchu	12 B 1	Tsitsa Bridge	12 D 3	Veekraal	21 C 4	Waverley	6 A 3		
Thaba Phatshwa	12 B 1	Tsitsing	18 A 1	Velddrif	4 B 1	Weenen	13 A 4	Zaaimansdal	5 C 6
Thabana Morena	12 C 1	Tsoelike	12 C 2	Velloor	9 A 4	Wegdraai	10 A 1	Zadungweni	12 D 2
Thabana	20 D 3	Tsolo	12 D 2	Ventersburg	18 D 1	Wegdraai	15 A 5	Zamani	18 D 3
Thabankulu	19 B 5	Tsomo	7 A 5	Ventersdorp	17 B 6	Weiveld	5 C 4	Zamdela	18 C 1
Thaba-Tseka	12 B 2	Tswaing	17 D 4	Venterspos	18 B 1	Welbedagtdam	11 B 6	Zanzibar	20 A 3
Thabazimbi	20 C 2	Tswaraganang	11 A 5	Venterstad	11 D 5	Welgeleë	17 D 6	Zaris	14 A 1
Thabong	17 D 6	Tswatago	21 C 4	Vereeniging	18 B 1	Welkom	17 D 6	Zastron	12 C 1
Thakazele	19 D 4	Tswelelang	17 C 5	Verena	20 D 3	Wellington	4 C 2	Zebediela Sta.	21 C 4
Thaleni	12 D 3	Tugela Ferry	13 A 4	Vergeleë	17 A 4	Welverdiend	15 A 5	Zebediela	21 C 4
Thamaga	20 A 1	Tugela Mouth	13 B 5	Vergesig	16 C 1	Welverdiend	16 C 1	Zebra	5 C 5
Thambokhulu	19 B 5	Tugela	13 B 5	Verkeerdevlei	12 A 1	Welverdiend	18 B 1	Zeekoegat	21 C 4
The Brook	19 B 4	Tuinplaas	20 D 3	Verkykerskop	18 D 2	Wembesi	13 A 4	Zeerust	17 A 5
The Cavern	12 A 3	Tulbagh	4 C 2	Vermaaklikheid	5 D 4	Wepener	12 B 1	Zenzeleni	18 D 2
The Crags	5 C 6	Tumahole	18 C 1	Vermaas	17 B 5	Werda	16 A 3	Zinkwazi Beach	13 B 5
The Haven	7 A 6	Turfbult	20 C 3	Vermont	4 D 2	Wesley	7 C 4	Zion City Moria	21 C 4
The Nest	12 A 3	Turton	13 C 4	Verulam	13 B 5	Wesselsbron	17 D 6	Zitapaleni	7 A 4
The Willows	6 C 2	Tutuka	18 C 3	Victoria Bay	5 C 5	Wesselton	18 B 3	Zitende	19 C 5
Thembalesizwe	6 B 1	Twee Rivier	15 A 5	Victoria West	10 D 3	Westerberg	10 B 2	Zithabiseni	18 A 2
Thembalethu	5 C 5	Twee Rivieren	15 B 6	Vierfontein	17 C 6	Westminster	12 B 1	Zithobeni	18 A 2
Thembalihle	18 C 3	Tweebuffels	17 B 6	Viljoensdrif	18 C 1	Westonaria	18 B 1	Zitundo	19 C 6
Thengwe	21 A 5	Tweefontein	12 B 1	Viljoenshof	4 D 2	Weza	12 C 3	Zoar	5 C 4
Theron	17 D 6	Tweefontein	20 D 3	Viljoenskroon	17 C 6	White Mountain	12 B 3	Zola	6 A 3
Theronsville	5 D 4	Tweefontein	4 A 2	Viljoenspos	19 D 4	White River	21 D 5	Zolani	4 C 3
Theunissen	11 A 6	Tweeling	18 D 2	Villa Nora	20 B 2	Whites	17 D 6	Zweletemba	4 C 2
Thixwadza	21 A 5	Tweespruit	12 B 1	Villiers	18 C 2	Whitesands	5 D 4	Zwelitsha	7 B 4
Thlakalatlou	16 D 3	Twenty Four Rivers	20 C 3	Villiersdorp	4 C 2	Whitmore	12 D 2		
Thohoyandou	21 B 5	Tyinindini	12 C 1	Vioolsdrif	8 A 2	Whittlesea	7 A 4		
Thokazi	19 D 5	Tylden	7 A 4	Virginia	17 D 6	Wiegnaarspoort	5 B 6		
Tholeni	13 A 4	Tzaneen	21 C 4	Visgat	20 C 2	Wilderness	5 C 5		
Thomas River	7 B 4			Vivo	21 B 4	Wilgenhoutsdrif	10 A 1		
Thombo	7 A 6	**U**		Vlakdrif	18 B 1	Willemsdal	18 C 2		
Thomeng	17 D 4			Vlaklaagte	20 D 3	Williston	9 D 6		
Thomo	21 B 5	Ubombo	19 D 6	Vlakplaas	18 C 2	Willowmore	5 C 6		
Thornham	6 C 1	Ugie	12 D 2	Vlakpoort	18 C 3	Willowvale	7 A 5		
Thornhill	6 A 3	Uitenhage	6 C 2	Vlakteplaas	5 C 5	Winburg	12 A 1		
Thornville	13 B 4	Uitkeer	6 B 2	Vlees Bay	5 D 5	Wincanton	16 D 2		
Three Sisters	5 A 6	Uitkomst	6 B 1	Vleidam	5 D 4	Wind Mill	4 C 2		
Tidbury's Toll	6 B 3	Uitsig	15 D 5	Vleiland	5 C 4	Windfield	18 C 2		
Tidimalo	11 A 4	Uitspankraal	4 A 2	Vleirivier	5 C 5	Windsorton Road	11 A 4		
Tierberg	9 A 6	Uitspanning	18 C 3	Vlieëkraal	17 D 5	Windsorton	17 D 4		
Tierfontein	17 D 6	Uitvlug	10 B 2	Vlieëkraal	4 A 3	Winterstrand	7 B 5		
Tierkloof	17 C 4	Uitvlugte	20 D 3	Voëlgeraas	10 C 3	Winterton	12 A 3		
Tigane	17 C 6	Uitweg	9 D 6	Volksrust	18 C 3	Wirsing	17 B 4		
Tikwana	17 D 5	Uitzicht	20 B 3	Volmoed	5 C 5	Witbank	18 B 3		
Timbavati Gate	21 C 5	Ulco	11 A 4	Volop	10 A 2	Witbank	8 A 3		
Tina Bridge	12 D 3	Ulundi	13 A 5	Volstruisleegte	5 B 6	Witbooisvlei	15 A 4		
Tinley Manor Beach	13 B 5	uMasizakhe	6 A 1	Volstruispan	18 A 2	Witdraai	15 C 6		
Tinmyne	20 C 3	Umbumbulu	13 C 4	Vondeling	5 C 6	Witfontein	20 C 2		
Tiptree	6 C 2	Umdloti Beach	13 B 5	Voorbaat	5 C 4	Withoogte	12 D 1		
Tjakastad	19 B 4	Umgababa	13 C 5	Voorreg	20 D 3	Witkleigat	17 A 5		
Tlapeng	16 C 3	Umgazi Mouth	7 A 6	Voorspoed	16 B 3	Witkop	11 D 6		
Tlaseng	20 D 2	uMhlali	13 B 5	Vorstershoop	16 B 2	Witmos	6 B 3		
Tlhabane	18 A 1	Umhlanga Rocks	13 B 5	Vosburg	10 C 2				

PHOTOGRAPHIC CREDITS

Cover:	– Shaen Adey
Page 7	– Roger de la Harpe
Page 8	– Pat de la Harpe
Page 13	– D. Allen / Photo Access
Page 37	– G. Whittal / Gallo Images
Page 39	– Roger de la Harpe
Page 41	– W. Knirr / Photo Access
Page 73	– D. Allen / Photo Access
Page 74	– P. Wagner / Photo Access

ACKNOWLEDGEMENTS:

We would like to thank all the relavent authorities for their help, information and material which enabled John Hall to compile and produce the cartography for this atlas. The Survey and Land Information office with their maps, aeronautical charts, aerial photography and Orthophoto maps were as always a great help.

80